Something
to Tell You

W9-AWS-729

BETWEEN MEN ~ BETWEEN WOMEN

LESBIAN AND GAY STUDIES

Lillian Faderman and Larry Gross, Editors

Something to Tell You

The Road Families

Travel When a

Child Is Gay

Gilbert Herdt and Bruce Koff

Columbia University Press NEW YORK

Columbia University Press

Publishers Since 1893

New York   Chichester, West Sussex

Copyright © 2000 Columbia University Press

Library of Congress Cataloging-in-Publication Data

Herdt, Gilbert H., *1949–*

Something to tell you : the road families travel when a child is gay /
Gilbert Herdt and Bruce Koff.

p.   cm.—(Between men—between women)

Includes bibliographical references and index.

ISBN 0–231–10438–3 (cloth)

ISBN 0–231–10439–1 (paper)

1. Parents of gays.   2. Gay youth—Family relationships.
3. Coming out (Sexual orientation)   I. Koff, Bruce.   II. Title.
III. Series.

HQ76.25.H44   1999

306.874—dc21   99–37669

Printed in the United States of America

Designed by Audrey Smith

c 10 9 8 7 6 5 4 3 2 1
p 10 9 8 7 6 5 4 3 2 1

Between Men ~ Between Women
Lesbian and Gay Studies

Lillian Faderman and Larry Gross, Editors

Advisory Board of Editors

CLAUDIA CARD
TERRY CASTLE
JOHN D'EMILIO
ESTHER NEWTON
ANNE PEPLAU
EUGENE RICE
KENDALL THOMAS
JEFFREY WEEKS

Between Men ~ Between Women is a forum for current lesbian and gay scholarship in the humanities and social sciences. The series includes both books that rest within specific traditional disciplines and are substantially about gay men, bisexuals, or lesbians and books that are interdisciplinary in ways that reveal new insights into gay, bisexual, or lesbian experience, transform traditional disciplinary methods in consequence of the perspectives that experience provides, or begin to establish lesbian and gay studies as a free-standing inquiry. Established to contribute to an increased understanding of lesbians, bisexuals, and gay men, the series also aims to provide through that understanding a wider comprehension of culture in general.

We dedicate this book with love to our partners and families for their constant love, generosity, and support:

To Gil's parents, Gilbert and Delores Herdt
To Gil's partner, Niels Teunis
To Niels's parents, Henk Teunis and Hennie Roelofs
To Bruce's parents, Robert and Vicki Koff
To Bruce's partner, Mitchell Channon
To Mitchell's parents, Vivian and Mayer Channon

Your children are not your children.
They are the sons and daughters of Life's longing for itself.
They come through you but not from you,
And though they are with you, yet they belong not to you.
You may give them your love but not your
thoughts.
For they have their own thoughts.
You may house their bodies but not their souls,
For their souls dwell in the house of tomorrow,
which you cannot visit, not even in your dreams.
You may strive to be like them, but seek not
to make them like you.
For life goes not backward nor tarries with
yesterday.
You are the bows from which your children
as living arrows are sent forth.
The archer sees the mark upon the path of
the infinite, and He bends you with His might
that His arrows may go swift and far.
Let your bending in the archer's hand be for
gladness;
For even as he loves the arrow that flies, so
He loves also the bow that is stable.

—Kahlil Gibran, *The Prophet*

Contents

Foreword

Where was this book when we needed it eleven years ago? When our son came out to us as gay and our daughter as lesbian, both within five months of each other, they got our attention. Fast. But we didn't know where to turn.

Like most parents of gays, we wondered what we had done to cause them to be "that way." We climbed our family trees, trying to remember any relatives, past or present, on my wife's side or mine, "who just might be, well, you know . . ." (we had trouble saying the H word). We talked with each other endlessly, and with our children at great length. We read everything we could get our hands on at the time about homosexuality—short of the embarrassment of checking books out of the public library (a silly thing to be embarrassed about, we know now).

When we found that a Parents, Families, and Friends of Lesbians and Gays (PFLAG) chapter met at a church nearby, we took courage and attended a meeting. We were surprised and pleased to find a lot of nice, normal people there, people much like us. We found the strength of those meetings in the shared experiences of other families. That is one of the strengths of this book as well. But like most parents and families, we needed more.

By sharing and evaluating a large variety of fascinating family accounts, Gilbert Herdt and Bruce Koff move in this book beyond mere stories into a deeply helpful realm of psychological and cultural understanding. Drawing upon the experiences of the parents they interviewed, they summarize those factors that tend to integrate and strengthen families and those that tend to cause separation and breakdown. They offer alternatives from which families can choose their own course.

Books such as this one and organizations such as PFLAG exist because our society does not yet accept and welcome lesbian, gay, bisexual, and transgendered children. Each of the more than 425 PFLAG chapters across the country exists as an oasis, a safe haven, an enclave where openness and unconditional love are the norm—characteristics that we believe will one day be true of our entire society. But until then, there are skilled counselors, welcoming communities of faith, PFLAG, and other local gay-friendly groups. And wonderfully helpful writers such as Gilbert Herdt and Bruce Koff.

Combining their personal experiences with their study of dozens of families, they point out how important it is to weave a lesbian or gay child into the fabric of his or her own household and, beyond it, into extended family relationships. They admit that sometimes conflicts may occur with those outside the family circle, but they show that integrated families are those who took the risk, held firm, and saw their courage pay off.

Our lesbian, gay, bisexual, and transgendered children live in a system that tends to dominate, control, and tyrannize them. Thus it tyrannizes all our families as well. It is a system the authors call the Heterosexual Family Myth. It teaches every child—falsely—that heterosexuality is the only normal sexual orientation. Few parents realize just how devastating this set of beliefs can be for children who are discovering themselves to be homosexual. The authors understand this well. For me, one of the most instructive parts of this book is the material on gay teens, who so often feel that they must reject and conceal a vital aspect of themselves in order to avoid rejection by others. Sadly, in many contexts these young people are right. As Herdt and Koff state, "The need to conceal the self becomes even more critical in the face of the violence and harassment so common in high school." The often abusive treatment meted out to lesbian, gay, bisexual, and transgendered persons, young and old, is based on false assumptions that take many forms and present many faces. Such assumptions have become a system perpetrated throughout our society and internalized by us all, even including gay people themselves and those of us in their families.

Yet the responses of many families in this study point toward overcoming difficulty with devotion. A variety of factors—experience in working through past crises, a healthy respect for differences, past exposure to gay people, finding supportive friends—can help families find their way, not only past the crisis but to new strength and a broader worldview. But of foremost importance, these writers found, is a refusal to be cowed. The families least likely to fare well were those who retreated into silence, treating their child's homosexuality as a shameful secret. They suffered deeply internalized oppression and sometimes the disintegration of the family into harmful patterns, including compromised relationships, distancing from others, deceitfulness, loss of closeness, and stunted maturity. The result was untold stress for all concerned.

You will read here of some religious families whose faith offers them strength in diversity. Yet for others, the religion to which they would turn is committed to silence and inactivity or even to teachings that condemn their children. Likewise, the military's "Don't ask, don't tell, don't pursue" farce is shown to be equally destructive, since gays are still being drummed out of the military, even while its leaders tolerate heterosexual adultery. How can we deal with this? The authors point out that homophobia does not have power over us unless we surrender to it. Gay people became homosexual in ways they did not choose and cannot control, just as heterosexuals neither choose nor can control their heterosexuality. But gays who are the victims of antigay propaganda—and we, their families—are nevertheless responsible for the way we respond. The web of homophobia can be broken as we learn to see homosexuality as it really is—simply another normal aspect of sexuality—and then describe that reality with the clarity of loving conviction.

Our goal is not just to free our loved ones from the tyranny of homophobia and the heterosexual family myth but to liberate all people to live in the light of full equality. As the authors ask, "What better lesson for America—a society challenged as never before by its diversity—than to see families, one by one, accepting and cherishing diversity?"

If you ask me, we are engaged in this commitment to real family values because it is exciting to strengthen our families and make them whole, because we have found stimulating ways to grow and expand our own horizons, and, frankly, because it's fun. We have new learning to do and new friends to make; we have support to give and deep appreciation to receive from our own kids, plus a few million more who value our standing boldly with them.

As Herdt and Koff conclude, "When parents choose to integrate their gay or lesbian child fully into their lives, they commit an act of love and heroism." In the process, we ourselves become liberated souls.

The Rev. Paul Beeman
National President, Parents, Families,
and Friends of Lesbians and Gays (PFLAG)

Preface

The story of this work begins with a large project conducted in Chicago. In 1987 anthropologist Gilbert Herdt, along with developmental psychologist Andrew Boxer and their colleagues at the University of Chicago, initiated a study of the identity development of gay and lesbian teenagers and their families and communities in the metropolitan area of Chicago that would continue until 1990. During this time, Bruce Koff served as director of Horizons Community Services, and his work and knowledge in this area led to the invitation to co-author this book. The project consisted of four separate but complementary studies: (1) a historical and ethnographic investigation of Chicago's north side "gay town" area, from 1910 to the present (directed by anthropologist Richard Herrell and assisted by Herdt); (2) an ethnographic study of a gay and lesbian social services agency, Horizons Community Services, Inc. (founded in 1973), which sponsors many lesbian/gay activities and support groups for lesbian/gay/bisexual teens in Chicago (directed by Herdt and assisted by graduate students at the University of Chicago); (3) a developmental identity study based upon interviews with 202 youth between the ages of thirteen and twenty, who represented the composite population of Chicago in terms of social class, ethnicity, religion, education, and other social factors (directed by Boxer, with the assistance of

Herdt, clinical psychologist Floyd Irvin, and graduate students from the University of Chicago); and (4) intensive interviews conducted with approximately fifty parents of lesbians and gays (directed by Boxer and assisted by Herdt). All responses were written, and the many quotes from parents in this book are derived from these responses.

In order to enhance our understanding of the ways in which culture, individuals, and families interact over time to create positive or negative mental health, social worker Bruce Koff and Gilbert Herdt also conducted follow-up interviews with youth and parents. We administered to each parent a semistructured interview and a battery of paper-and-pencil tests that would reveal to us the parents' thinking and life experiences and enable us to assess their mental health. We wished to examine in particular the parents' processes of coping with a child's coming out. *Something to Tell You* is based upon these interviews with parents of lesbian and gay children.

What kinds of parents were these? They ranged in age from their late thirties to their seventies, with an average age of sixty. They were middle-class as well as working-class people. In most cases, their sons and daughters had come out to them during young adulthood. The average length of time since the children had disclosed their homosexuality to their parents was five years prior to the interview, and the range was from less than one year to more than ten years. Unlike the subjects of other studies of this kind, none of the parents were seen in clinical situations. Generally, they were no different from parents in average families. None of them were so disrupted that their lives could not go on. We located them primarily through the Chicago chapter of Parents, Families, and Friends of Lesbians and Gays (PFLAG) and the Horizons Community Services program for Gay, Lesbian, and Bisexual Teens. However, we were also fortunate to be able to interview some parents who shunned any public group that would draw attention to them as parents of lesbians and gays. We believe that as a result of our interviews with a diversity of parents we can help shed new light on the struggle to integrate gay and lesbian children into ordinary families.

While the cultural identities of "gay" and "lesbian" are not universal—and, therefore, the stories in this book do not apply to the experiences of people in all times and places—nevertheless their significance holds for parents of gays and lesbians in the industrialized and urban areas of the United States and Western Europe. Our cross-cultural work and our work in Holland, where Gilbert Herdt has taught and conducted institutes and collaborated in research with Dutch colleagues for some years, convinces us that the American experience of the parents of gays and lesbians has parallels in Western European centers.

The realization that a child is gay or lesbian can plunge a family into a dilemma they may never have anticipated. A door is flung open, and parents, not knowing what lies beyond, can only choose whether or not to walk through it to the future. This book is primarily about parents who have made the passage. Our interviews with them have enabled us to detail the challenges they have faced, the decisions they have made, the strategies they have employed, and some surprising rewards they have garnered as a result.

What actually happens to the family as a result of learning that a son or daughter is gay? How is the parents' marriage affected? Is the self-esteem of the parents affected? How do relationships with brothers and sisters change? How does communication change? What impact does the disclosure have on the integrity of the individual members of a family? As we sought to answer these questions by analyzing our interviews with parents of lesbians and gays, we discerned often a healthy sequence in the developmental responses to a child's disclosure. Many of the stories parents tell in this book suggest that we should think of how families cope with having a gay child as a long process—as if they are embarking on a difficult voyage in very stormy seas. To negotiate the trip successfully requires a map and a very sturdy vessel—solid and stable family bonds. There are many travails on such a voyage, but if all goes well, the vessel can hope to arrive safely in port and, perhaps, even be better off for the passage.

As a significant number of the parents that we interviewed have concluded, once they embraced their gay or lesbian child, they experienced immensely positive changes in key aspects of their lives: Marital relationships and family bonds were strengthened, better relations with friends were fostered, and the parents felt an improvement in their own self-esteem. *Something to Tell You* is their story of how such positive changes came about.

The primary purpose of this book is to address the needs of parents of gays and lesbians, as well as the professionals and caring others who are in positions to be of support to them. Why is such a book necessary? Because the issue of gay and lesbian children in the family is fraught with complexity. Our research and clinical work has convinced us of two things: (1) gays and lesbians are too often unprepared to handle the conflicts with their parents and families that stem from their coming out, and (2) parents are unprepared for the painful and difficult steps that will lead them from the shock and denial of their initial reactions to a discovery of how to integrate their lesbian or gay child fully back into the family. The rules of how to behave in the situation—for example, how to negotiate the child's coming out to the extended family—have not been formulated. While part of the deficit may lie in us as individuals, it surely resides largely in our culture. In fact, we would argue that it is generally not the gay or lesbian child who is impaired or the family that is flawed; rather, as we will discuss in chapter 2, it is the society that is handicapped by a cultural myth that has outlived its usefulness and time.

Despite the tenacious existence of that cultural myth, we believe that legislative, judicial, and personal changes that will bring about a better and more decent America—one in which stigma and discrimination against lesbians and gays and their families will be no more—are soon to come and merit continued support. It is our hope that this book will succeed not only in opening up a new conversation about what a good family life can be and helping parents to embrace their gay and lesbian children but also in breaking down prejudice and helping to put an end to a cultural myth that retains the power to be destructive.

Acknowledgments

This book would not have been possible without the support of many colleagues and friends, as well as several institutions, over a period of years. For support of the original research on which this book is based, we should like to thank the Spencer Foundation of Chicago and, in particular, Linda May Fitzgerald and Nancy Foster. The grant was made to Gilbert Herdt (Principal Investigator) and Andrew Boxer, (Project Director) for the project, "Cultural Competence and Sexual Orientation: A Study of Adolescence in Chicago." Additional support for data analysis came from grants of the Biomedical Research Fund of the Social Sciences Division, University of Chicago. The writing of this book was completed while Gilbert Herdt was supported by a Guggenheim Fellowship and The Robert S. Vaughn Visiting Fellowship at the Robert Penn Warren Center for the Humanities, Vanderbilt University. We are especially grateful to the late Andrew Boxer, our colleague and friend, who was the director of the original study and collaborated in the collection and analysis of these data and has supported our effort to make this work public.

We would like to praise again our field director, Rachelle Ballmer, whose intelligence, good cheer, and dedication made our project possible. We would also like to thank psychologist Dr. Floyd Irvin, anthropologist Richard Herrell, and psychologist Lisa Pickens for their research support, and Mark Tegenfeldt for technical support.

We are very grateful to our colleagues who conducted the fine detailed interviews necessary to the success of the early project: Rachelle Ballmer, Andrew Boxer, Jerry Olson, Valerie Glover, Elizabeth Davies, Mary Olmstead, and Amy Blumenthal.

We are grateful to several friends and colleagues for support of the early project, and wish especially to thank sociologist Judith Cook and psychoanalyst Bertram Cohler.

Our friends at PFLAG (Parents, Families, and Friends of Lesbians and Gays) deserve a hearty thanks for their help in this study. We would like to offer special praise to Mayer and Vivian Channon, who were extremely helpful. We are grateful for their friendship and support. We also thank Gerda Muri and Nancy Johnson for their kindness.

For their reading and comments on this book, we would like to offer our appreciation and gratitude to Caitlin Ryan, Andy Boxer, Harlie Ezgur, and Linda Meyers.

Finally, for her gracious and kind patience and keen eye, we offer warm thanks to our editor, Ann Miller, at Columbia University Press.

Something to Tell You

Introduction

When Your Child Says,
"I Have Something
to Tell You . . ."

I had never known anybody who was gay
before. It was like the bottom of the world
dropped out. I loved him and was so proud he
had done well; but it was like a death in the
family and I couldn't talk to anyone.

—*Flora, sixty-eight-year-old mother of a gay son*

EVEN NOW, AT THE END OF THE TWENTIETH CENTURY, it is still very difficult to stand up and say, "I am a parent of a gay child." Parents are generally unprepared to deal with the profound challenge of having a gay son or lesbian daughter. When the child declares, "I have something to tell you . . . I'm gay," it often feels to a parent as though a dream is shattered. As the mother of a gay son said to us: "At first I think I was disappointed, because you do have dreams. He's a shining Adonis—so of course we had dreams. It's hard to bury those dreams!" Yet, as we discovered in our interviews with parents, those who can learn to integrate their gay and lesbian children into their families often find unexpected, rich rewards.

The Burton Family's "Integration"

Mark and Peggy Burton (all names and identifying information have been changed throughout this book, in order to preserve the anonymity of the interview subjects) were married in their early twenties and moved quickly toward creating a family. Peggy gave birth to Julie one year later, and four years after that brought Joey into the world. Unfortunately, Mark and Peggy lapsed into an increasingly joyless relationship, burdened by the pressures of children and finances. As Peggy's dissatisfaction grew, so did her drinking. As a result, she acknowledges now, she was not fully available to her children. Peggy and Mark divorced when Julie was fourteen years old and Joey was ten. Peggy also got sober, entered a recovery program, and focused more on her children.

Peggy described her daughter Julie as having been a "bright and special" child. Julie excelled academically and athletically, and, not surprisingly, she gained admission to an Ivy League college. Julie's accomplishments reassured Peggy that her children had managed to overcome the potentially devastating effects of her troubled marriage and painful divorce and her years as an active alcoholic.

So it was a tremendous shock when Julie called her mother from college and told her that she was involved with another woman. As Peggy described it, "I wish the Earth could have opened and swallowed me up!" Like so many parents, she struggled between blaming herself and blaming others. "I wanted to fly out there and beat up whoever it was that I thought was seducing her." Then Peggy thought, "I'd done it to her. For the first trimester (of my pregnancy with Julie) I bled intermittently and was given progesterone. . . . I thought I'd altered her sexuality with the hormones."

Peggy was so shocked by Julie's disclosure that she couldn't talk to her. "I just cut her out. I felt irate, but instead of talking, I blocked it out . . . totally denied it. I wanted to believe she was being pursued and was only concerned about hurting this person's feelings by being too rejecting."

Peggy wanted for Julie what most mothers want for their daughters: for her "to meet a wonderful man who would love her—a vine-covered cottage with three children, a flourishing career with theatrical work on the side. I wanted her to have everything." Julie's disclosure precipitated what Peggy describes as "a period of severe depression."

Now, however, Peggy embraces Julie's sexual orientation as "just another piece of information." She has a close and communicative relationship with her daughter and has welcomed Julie's lover into her home. She is proud of Julie and proud of herself.

How Peggy Burton progressed from a state of devastation to a relationship of comfort and pride was a result of the process we call "integration," by which we mean the rejoining of a missing element to the whole. As we describe in subsequent chapters, the stigma associated with homosexuality, and the concomitant fear associated with it, often compel the gay or lesbian child and his or her family to separate or to deny any parts of the child's life and personality that could reveal a homosexual identity. The subsequent "disintegration" is insidious and often devastating to the family. However, the disintegration may be reversed. Through our interviews with parents, we have found that when the missing pieces are woven back into the family, the fabric is strengthened. The family affirms its own "integrity"—a term that the dictionary defines as "the quality or condition of being whole or undivided; completeness."

The Cost of Not Integrating

We all grow up with a variety of notions about what it means to be gay and lesbian: what gay and lesbian people do, how they came to be "that way," how they live, how they relate to others, and even how they age and die. All of these derive from the pervasive idea around which our society is organized, an idea we call the Heterosexual Family Myth. By "Myth" we do not mean an ancient story or a deception so much as an ideal theme that embodies our culture and guides us in organizing our beliefs and actions. The Heterosexual Family Myth is thus a cultural ideal. It embodies a set of expectations for how one's life should unfold. Unfortunately, it is uncompromising. It insists that only through heterosexual union and the bearing of children within such a union can all happiness and positive meaning be achieved. It implies that deviation from this path is less meaningful, less worthy of social approval, less fulfilling, and, ultimately, less happy.

Thus, having been imbued with the Myth, almost all parents in our study described their initial disappointment in learning that their child was lesbian or gay. Often they expressed their disappointment in the context of not having grandchildren, since, for them as for most older parents, grandchildren represent the fulfillment of the Myth—a crowning achievement to a life dedicated to the ideal of heterosexuality. Of course, lesbians and gay men are increasingly choosing to have children through adoption and donor insemination. But despite this fairly recent development, the fear that they will never be grandparents was disheartening to most of the parents that we interviewed, as we will discuss in chapter 1. More significantly, how the parents learned to confront the Myth—and how they went about building a new culture that could ameliorate the old legacy of confusion and pain left to them by an ideal that is no longer relevant to their lives—constitutes a crucial element in *Something to Tell You.*

The concept of a gay or lesbian "identity" is very recent by historical standards. It is hard to believe that the notion of "the homosexual" emerged only about 1870. In earlier eras it was thought that anyone might *behave* homosexually (and some societies approved while others disapproved). But there was no concept of *the homosexual* as a category of persons. The nineteenth-century invention of "the homosexual" as being a person apart from other people led soon to the creation in our culture of a new "spoiled identity," as the sociologist Erwin Goffman once called it. Our society now demeans lesbians and gay men through hate, discrimination, and violence. Families with gay or lesbian offspring must confront this unfortunate legacy, for as a child "comes out" (proclaims his or her homosexuality) to parents, hoping to be affirmed, the parents ironically find their own identity suddenly "spoiled" by having a gay or lesbian child.

It is easy enough to identify the various risks of accepting the gay or lesbian child's special identity and integrating him or her into the family. For many families, the price that a path of integration exacts may be too high. For example, telling the grandparents may be "too much for them to handle." Parents may risk ridicule or pity from friends for publicly embracing their lesbian daughter and her lover. Disclosing that a family has a gay or lesbian child may cause other relatives and acquaintances to question the parent's effectiveness or even cause them to question the parent's own sexual orientation. Accepting and supporting a gay or lesbian child may also place the parents at odds with their own church, mosque, or synagogue.

Since the challenge of fully acknowledging that a child is gay or lesbian and integrating him or her into a family is frequently arduous and daunting, why pursue the idea at all? Why can't we simply agree to ignore it, to adapt the "Don't Ask, Don't Tell" policy of the U.S. military to relationships with our children, so that we, too, can just get along? Because the inability or the failure to pursue an integrated path may have hidden costs that are far more lasting and damaging to the family.

In her book *The Family Heart: A Memoir of When Our Son Came Out*, Robb Forman Dew passionately describes her own horror at the "atrocity" of silence with which so many parents respond initially to the subject of homosexuality: "We unknowingly let our children grow up in a society that reflects back at them utter scorn for their legitimate emotions. And if our children look to us for confirmation or denial of their dawning understanding of how hard their lives might be, they are met with nothing but a lethal silence, or worse—our unwitting but implied concurrence."[1]

Many researchers note that parents' rejection or intolerance of their child's sexual orientation can significantly diminish the child's self-esteem and capacity to function effectively in life. As one author characterized this, gay or lesbian children, compelled to limit their disclosures to the family, "become half-members of the family unit, afraid and alienated, unable ever to be totally open and spontaneous, to trust or be trusted, to develop a fully socialized sense of self-affirmation. This sad stunting of human potential breeds stress for gay people and their families alike—stress characterized by secrecy, ignorance, helplessness and distance."[2] Gay and lesbian adolescents are particularly vulnerable to the loss of parental support in their battle to integrate their sexual orientation. Recent studies have shown that the average age today of first same-sex fantasies and experiences is quite young, perhaps even younger than a generation ago. In our own study of gay and lesbian youth, the average age of first same-sex attraction was 9.6 years for boys, and 10.1 years for girls. The average age of first same-sex experience was 13.1 years for boys and 13.6 years for girls.[3] As one researcher notes, "Compared to older persons, early and middle adolescents may be generally less able to cope with the isolation and stigma of a homosexual identity." They desperately need parental support. The cost of not getting such support may be grave. As other studies have shown, gay and lesbian youth are at greater risk for suicide, homelessness, and substance abuse than other young people. Indeed, one federally funded study found that 25 percent of street youth may be gay or lesbian.[4]

A family's failure to fully integrate the life of its lesbian or gay child, regardless of the child's age, will fragment and overburden the lives of all concerned. Gay or lesbian adult children may determine that it is better to move far away from the family and thus avoid the complications of incorporating a lover or life partner within the family system. Others may be so willing to accommodate themselves to their parents' conditional acceptance that they may consciously or unconsciously avoid involvement in lasting or committed same-sex relationships. Parents may thus be spared the humiliation they associate with having a homosexual child—and the child avoids the discomfort of "causing" this pain to the family or, worse, triggering a complete break with the family. But the cost to the child of such denial is tremendous.

Early in development, gay or lesbian children may exhibit accommodation behavior that can be crippling. It can lead to their habitually assuming codependent roles or people-pleasing behaviors within all later relationships. In effect, the gay or lesbian person concludes, "The only way for me to ensure that others will not reject me is to do whatever the other person wants and be whatever the other person wants me to be." The results of such an approach to intimate relationships can be disastrous. Generally, it is impossible to please others in this way. Power becomes so unequally distributed within relationships that it generates immense resentment as well. The tendency toward self-destructive accommodation can be so deeply rooted that it can render an individual more vulnerable to abuse within his or her romantic and sexual relations in later life.

Even in nonromantic relationships, such as those with friends or colleagues at work, the effects of this accommodation dynamic can be profound. Often, individuals who so readily accommodate others, who say "Yes," when really they feel "No," wind up exploited and feeling chronically overburdened. In work settings, they may rise rapidly in a hierarchy that promotes the "dedicated" worker who is willing to leave little room in life for anything else but work, and stress or burnout invariably follow.

Some gay and lesbian children will even internalize and reflect the homophobia they find within the responses of their parents. Each "fag joke" a parent or sibling utters, every epithet or derisive comment made about lesbians or gay men, is a wound to the heart of gay or lesbian children. They experience the self as the target of these seemingly casual cruelties, whether or not the cruelties are directed specifically at them. It is even more cruel when the comments *are* directed against the child. The brother who taunts his sister for looking like a "dyke," the father who mocks his son for acting like a "fairy," both contribute to a gay or lesbian child's propensity toward depression, self-hatred, and self-destructiveness.

Gay or lesbian children may develop a very limited view of themselves in response to family hostility. For example, they may feel unworthy of another's love or seek ways to dispel a sense of unworthiness through addictive or self-destructive means. Michelangelo Signorile, in his recent analysis of gay male culture, draws a stark relationship between the impaired self-esteem of gay men and a core element of gay male culture that fosters self-destructive behavior in a drive for affirmation.[5] He notes that the use of drugs, the pursuit of the "perfect body," the desperate wish to be the object of desire even to the point of risking HIV infection, are all potential manifestations of alienation and insufficient feelings of self-worth. He argues that homophobia engenders within some gay men the notion that they are only of value as a sexual object. Others may feel limited to certain careers or feel condemned to failure. While there may be significant differences between how lesbians and gay men cope with these psychological wounds, both populations appear to be at risk for further harm as a consequence of being wounded. With such a legacy of pain, it is no wonder that gay and lesbian teens may be two to three times more likely to attempt suicide than their heterosexual counterparts.[6]

When families reinforce the shame and stigma associated with homosexuality by their rejection, silence, or even limited tolerance for that aspect of their child's identity, they risk further disabling the developmental process of both individual and family resilience and growth. Gay or lesbian children may direct what they perceive as hatred back toward themselves: denying deepest feelings and desires or condemning themselves for having them; or—most tragic of all—rejecting themselves completely through the act of suicide. Such are the potential destructive costs to children when families stumble on the path toward integration.

But what are the hidden costs to parents when they feel compelled to conceal a child's sexual orientation? As surely as the gay son or daughter exits a "closet" by coming out to parents—so this very act of disclosure creates a "closet" for the parents. They must now decide whether or not to "come out" as parents of a lesbian daughter or gay son. Not doing so can produce effects that are parallel to those their children have faced. Parents, like their gay and lesbian children, may also internalize a sense of shame or failure. Those who pride themselves on living honorably and honestly may find themselves deeply compromised by the sudden need to deceive others or conceal such a critical change in their lives. Each time parents seek to steer a discussion with their peers away from areas that may reveal their child's sexual orientation, each time they gloss over details or inflate the child's accomplishments in one area in order to deny their disappointment in another area, they distance themselves in their relationships from others. They lose faith in the closeness of family as well as friends.

We learned repeatedly through the parents that we interviewed about the difference it can make in the lives of all family members to choose the path of integration. For parents it is freeing in positive and unexpected ways. The inability of families to integrate their gay or lesbian child fully can inhibit the normal processes of maturation and growth so crucial to the child's development into a fully functioning adult. That inhibition has a tremendous impact on parents since, as children mature and embark on their journey outward toward a more autonomous life, parents can normally expect to relinquish much of the parental role. For parents the child's maturation begins a time to rediscover self-identity anew because the parental identity recedes into the background. The care-taking parent may choose to return to school or resume a career. The working parent may pursue a new hobby or shift to a more relaxed work setting or schedule. The parents may wish to take advantage of their newfound freedom from the constraints of child-rearing by travelling together. But when the child fails to mature fully, the parents cannot easily relinquish their roles as parents. Parents cannot obtain a sense of accomplishment and enjoy a satisfying and fulfilling transition to life beyond the "empty nest."

When the child does "come out," however, the parents have an opportunity to work through more successfully the developmental tasks associated with "letting go" of children as they create more autonomous lives of their own. And ironically, as many of the parents in integrated families report, the closeness, devotion, and love between family members is enhanced. Seeing each other as separate, whole, and complete individuals allows the family to hold to each other by choice, respect, and love, rather than by obfuscation, shame, and denial.

Most of the parents in our study were anxious to share their experiences because they have learned so much from having a gay or lesbian child. Many saw this study as an opportunity to encourage and support other parents, to say: "Look! We've found a way to deal with this. What we once thought of as a terrible burden has become a gift. Listen to us. We have something to tell you."

What they tell us is that parenting today is an art, as much as it is a skill. Child-rearing in modern American society requires parents to acknowledge the separateness of children, to value difference in them and the world around them, and to foster the growth of their unique talents and spirit. They may not always know what to do as parents, they say, but they must always approach the task by listening to their hearts. And at the heart of most parents is the capacity to appreciate truly the unique identities of their gay or lesbian children, whether they know of this distinction early on, as some of our parents did, or discover this difference much later. It is through such open-hearted love that families transcend what often appears to them initially to be the crisis of having a lesbian or gay child.

The challenge to parents ought never to be whether to love your gay or lesbian child, but how. Even the National Conference of Catholic Bishops emphasized this point in its recent pastoral message, "Always Our Children." They state: "Your child may need you and the family now more than ever. He or she is still the same person. This child, who has always been God's gift to you, may now be the cause of another gift: your family becoming more honest, respectful and supportive."[7] Learning that a child is gay or lesbian need not lead to the all-too-frequent battle between the parents and the child. There is, in fact, a vital battle that must be waged instead—a reckoning between the family as a whole and the intolerant culture around it that seeks to undermine the family because it embraces gay or lesbian children and those they love.

In our study it was not always the words of parents that spoke so eloquently of love but, rather, their actions. Particularly for those parents that were well along the path toward integration, love was active. They not only responded to their child lovingly and supportively when the child came out to them; they also went an extra step. They purchased books, read articles, talked to supportive and knowledgeable therapists and clergy, attended meetings of a national organization, Parents, Families, and Friends of Lesbians and Gays (PFLAG), befriended other parents of gays and lesbians, and met and became familiar with local lesbian and gay communities. They often allowed their gay children to take the lead in educating them about a new world of which they knew little. They drew inspiration and pride from the courage of these gay children. As a result, important changes often occurred. Primarily, parents learned to "let go" in various ways: to let go of the Myth that only through heterosexual relationships can families and individuals find fulfillment, as well as its corollary, that having gay or lesbian children can only lead to loss, alienation, and shame; to let go of the children themselves, so that those children can resume their developmental path; and to let go of the parental role enough to determine freely their own next step in life, having successfully launched their children into responsible adulthood.

Many of these parents told us in the interviews that they now enjoyed a deepening of family ties. Couples who shared this active approach to growing and changing found new strength in their marital relationships and greater peace and optimism. With such revitalization these families could expand the circle of love to embrace others. For some, this meant disclosing their child's sexual orientation to extended family. For others, it meant welcoming their lesbian daughter's partner or gay son's lover and the families of those partners and lovers into their own family.

A number of the parents we interviewed also committed themselves to challenging the very culture that stigmatizes them and their children. Some became leaders in PFLAG in their effort to educate others. Other parents spoke out in their own churches or synagogues, or challenged friends who casually disparaged lesbians or gay men. Each such act of outspokenness reinforced the integrity of the family and its members. In effect, the parents in our study who sought integration have turned the argument about "family values" on its head. To them, it is not homosexuality that constitutes a "threat" to families but the shame and stigma others associate with it. By integrating their gay or lesbian children rather than rejecting them, these families found they functioned better than they ever had before. Through the lessons of their experience, the parents in our study call upon all parents of gays and lesbians to respect their children as unique individuals; to treasure those qualities that make them unique, including their homosexual orientation; to love actively; to let go; to draw strength from their children and from each other; to expand the circle of love; and hence to challenge a society that undermines the family by attaching shame and stigma to the gift of having a child who happens to be lesbian or gay.

These parents' call is made achievable by their example, which gives us a model of faith in family that is more sure than any outmoded Myth and that is as real as love itself. Parents who have done the work, who have made the fabric whole, have learned that the experience of integrating a gay or lesbian child into the family was like a special gift that came to them in the second half of their lives. These parents likened the process to opening a door on a world never discovered before. It is our hope that readers of this book will find in it a similar process of discovery.

1

The Heterosexual Family Myth

How It Can Be Harmful

This is just not the way it is [supposed] to be
... [My gay son] has interrupted my whole
life. It's not in the plan. Kids have kids. ... In
the time I was born, first you are someone's
daughter, then you are someone's wife, and
then mother, grandmother, and so on. Cradle to grave.

—*Margot, forty-one-year-old mother*
of a gay son

I mean, we're taught to think that's not a normal way of life. We think in terms of procre-
ating—that's normal. I said that to my son,
and he said, "It is a normal way of life—to
me." Well, yes, it's normal to him, but it isn't
mainstream.

—*Mary, sixty-two-year-old mother of a gay son*

WHAT GOES THROUGH A PARENT'S MIND WHEN A CHILD SAYS "I have something to tell you"? Whether their offspring is nine or thirty-nine, parents know that this moment of revelation will bring surprises—and not all of them are wanted. Yet such a highly significant moment has the potential to be very positive, since the parent has been taken into the confidence of a loving child who is going to share a secret. In fact, for many offspring, sharing in this way is truly a burst of brave love—a breakthrough of self-confidence, a move toward maturity in the parent-child relationship, a yearning to be accepted as unique and to be true to the self. But when the shared secret concerns a child's homosexuality, it may have the effect of interrupting the life of the parent by disrupting the myths and notions of the ideal family. What are the particular cultural myths that provoke such uncomfortable reactions in parents? How do those myths influence the ability of parents to integrate their gay and lesbian children successfully into their families?

The Heterosexual Family Myth

"Myth," as we mean the term in this chapter, does not necessarily connote a lie or a deception; nor do we mean to imply that heterosexual families don't really exist. Rather, we use the term "Myth" in the anthropological sense: myths provide a powerful guiding image or a map—a central tendency—for the organization of the individual lifecourse and the goals and conduct of social life in the community. A myth, in this sense of a cultural story, is thus a plan for what individuals should strive to achieve in society. Rituals and ceremonies within the culture reinforce the importance of the myth. In our society, we might regard engagement parties, weddings, baby showers, and anniversary parties as rituals that reinforce the cultural ideal of the heterosexual family. No society can sustain itself without an appeal to myths of this kind. Ours is no different.

But what is the impact of this Myth on the lives of families of gays and lesbians? We believe that the Myth as it is spun in the media and daily life excludes many people, and specifically we want to show how it has excluded families of gays and lesbians along with gays and lesbians themselves. Our attention to what we call the Heterosexual Family Myth stems from our effort to understand the stories of parents who have told us what it is like to discover that their child is homosexual. To be heterosexual and married with children is statistically normal. But it is a culturally pervasive belief that *only* heterosexuals who are married and have children are "perfectly normal." This is one of the most powerful myths in our lives and our society. Indeed, most people grow up feeling that to be married and have children is the cornerstone of their development throughout life. Rearing their family with these same expectations, organizing their hopes and dreams around seeing their children grow up and marry, parents look forward to the day when they will be grandparents. This American cultural ideal of the normal heterosexual family may work fine for the majority of people. But those who deviate from the majority are condemned by our society because they are deemed not "normal."

While there is much to commend the Heterosexual Family Myth, ultimately it fails to satisfy the desires and designs of many people in our society, simply because they are different. They cannot abide by the Myth, which has no power to make them happy. The Myth stigmatizes their difference as "abnormal" or "flawed." Many gays and lesbians thus are made to *feel* abnormal or flawed in our society. Their parents, likewise, are made to feel abnormal or flawed since the way children are (their nature and being) is often seen to reflect back upon their parents, and the parents in turn may regard the differences in the child as shortcomings in themselves.

Roberta, a fifty-three-year-old mother of five, with a twenty-nine-year-old gay son, is a case in point. She now expresses high admiration for her son, and she and her husband of thirty-four years are in a solid and affectionate relationship with him. In fact, she feels strongly that dealing with her son's homosexuality has made her a better person. But she went through a great deal of grief before she was able to feel that way. It seems that much of her grief had to do with the Heterosexual Family Myth.

As she recalled in our interview, "I would have liked for [my son] to get married and have a child because he was such a beautiful baby. Sure, [I experienced] both disappointments and readjustments. It's hard to remember because it was such a nightmare. I had such a fear of telling friends and family because I was such a perfect mother. Then this flaw came into the picture. I was no longer the perfect mother."

Roberta had believed that to be a "perfect mother" is to have a "perfect baby," who should, of course, turn out to be heterosexual. The "flaw" that Roberta spoke of is nothing but the absence of heterosexuality in her son. How were Roberta and her husband able to transcend this conviction that their son's homosexuality was a "flaw"? The key to their success had to do with their realization that their love for their son was, indeed, unconditional.

Conditional affection is not love. Children who know that parental affection is conditional may even come to feel that they will only be loved if they contribute to the ideal of the perfect heterosexual family. This presents a terrible dilemma for the gay son and lesbian daughter. The developing gay or lesbian child assumes, "There is something wrong with me," or "I have a secret to hide." As the child matures into adolescence, she or he begins to think, "My parents don't know who I really am." If children, rightly or wrongly, believe that their parents will despise or reject them if they disclose their homoerotic feelings, then they will do everything possible to hide those "bad" feelings. They have difficulty shaking the conviction that "if they really did know me, they wouldn't love me anymore." The sense of imperfect and conditional love necessitates disintegration: hiding that part of the self believed to be unlovable and disclosing only the lovable part. Throughout the many years of hiding and fear of rejection, children may nourish a small hope that somehow, someday, they will be able to come out to their parents and still be loved. But they don't count on it. Coming out is thus typically postponed until well into adulthood.

A commonly shared stereotype, the Heterosexual Family Myth acts as a critical barrier to the formation of more realistic and loving relations between parents and their gay and lesbian offspring. Our society's pat definition of "normality" leads to pervasive expectations concerning the "normal heterosexual child." But the gay or lesbian person simply cannot fulfill the cultural expectations. As a consequence, family members feel shame, fear, and failure. They are victimized by our modern theory of "human nature," which tells what is "normal" and what is "abnormal." It is the culture that inhibits the integration of gays and lesbians into their families.

The Heterosexual Family Myth is a collective cultural myth that attempts to encompass *everyone in the world*. Like myths in many times and places, this one functions to charter institutions—particularly marriage, the nuclear family (a biological father, mother, and child), and gender roles for men and women. The Myth also functions to explain the necessity of conforming in order to be "normal." It hints at apocalyptic events and imposes sanctions should people break the norm—insanity, criminality, the loss of love and family support, the denial of acceptance and standing in the community, and a panoply of other dark outcomes. The cultural ideal of heterosexuality purports that simply by being heterosexual, the child will be happy. The powerful norms and roles that emerge from the cultural ideal bind people to the social fabric, captivating the energies and fantasies of the individual by turning social norms into personal aspirations. Myths thus exert powerful social controls over the development of us all, directing people along the same path, with the same kinds of goals and aspirations.

All of us grow up, as many people we interviewed observed, with a guiding image of what it means to be a normal and healthy human being. As we suggested earlier, when we refer to that image as a "Myth," we do not mean to say that it is false or unreal; nor is it our intention to disparage or dismiss this powerful and cherished dream around which many people build their whole lives. But we do wish to point out injustices and falsities: the Myth and the sanctions it imposes on differences are often so grave and stigmatizing that families with gay or lesbian offspring who, by definition, deviate from the Myth face public rejection and exile from the larger community.

In addition, the Myth excludes from the table all of humanity (whether straight or gay) that does not fulfill its inflexible demands: its outcasts are heterosexuals who choose not to have children; gay men and lesbians; those who are divorced and separated; blended families; and so on. Regardless of contemporary realities that make such deviance common, this Myth is still the building block of socialization: it is taught in families and schools, as well as through television, books, and the myriad stories of our culture. The incessant message tells how by falling in love with someone of the opposite sex and desiring to have children with the beloved (the greatest expression of love) a person achieves normal development and happiness. Something is abnormal or wrong with a boy or girl who does not get married, stay married, and have children, according to the formula of this sacred Myth.

And yet, it is impossible for anyone not to see that society has changed in many ways that challenge the cultural stereotypes of the normal heterosexual family promoted by the media and our society. There are now many different lifestyles that do not match the norms of the past. Our postindustrial service-sector economy has made it economically difficult, even undesirable, for most individuals to have large families. The diversity of people and behavior in the United States has made us aware that there is no single formula for successful adaptation or development. What our liberal democracy holds dear is the ability to accept and fold into its society divergent ways of life.

The popular television series of today reflect this pivotal historical change. "Roseanne" discovers that her mother is a lesbian, and "Murphy Brown" chooses to be a professional career woman and a single parent. The significant media attention directed to the television show *Ellen*, which depicted the coming out of the character played by Ellen DeGeneres, strongly prodded the debate on exposure of children and adolescents to such issues. Painful and funny as some of these media images are, they represent quite powerful challenges to the old Myth. But it is important to note that the cultural ideal for families and individuals remains intact even as it fades. Ironically, parents could have once relied upon the bias of others to keep the secrets intact too, or to reassure them that their own prejudices regarding their gay and lesbian children were morally correct. That is no longer true.

What has happened is that the consensus in our society is breaking down about the myth of heterosexuality, just as the concomitant negative stereotypes of homosexuality are changing. It is no longer the case that people are necessarily ashamed to be gay or lesbian; they may in fact be proud of it. Even celebrities and politicians may be openly gay. Indeed, the social movement of gays, lesbians, and bisexuals celebrates divergent sexuality as pride: it is simply another, equally valued form of "diversity"—of human nature, albeit different in kind. The recent debate in the country over gays and lesbians in the military is a serious demonstration of a new kind of political and social force alive in the United States. "Don't ask, don't tell, don't pursue" is a policy that comprised a variety of positions and will surely not last, but the controversy around it definitely represents a profound questioning of the cultural ideal of the Myth that only heterosexuality is normal and that homosexuality is unworthy—even in the military.

Simultaneously, other segments of our society have changed. It is no longer unusual to find heterosexual couples who are living together but who are unmarried; or divorced and separated couples, whose children are being reared in single-parent households. Career women and their husbands increasingly decide to postpone or delay the decision to have children, or to adopt them, or not to have children at all. Often these decisions are disappointments to their parents, but parents are learning how to cope with them. Indeed, the idea of gender equality for women in the workplace has made the whole issue of children and grandchildren more complicated than before.

Nevertheless, there remains a strong tendency for our culture to lean upon the legacy of the past, such as idealized images from the nineteenth century and an earlier part of the twentieth century. Perhaps the strongest images of heterosexism (i.e., the culturally conditioned belief that heterosexuality is inherently superior to homosexuality) were the ones on millions of television sets of the 1950s and 1960s— the period in which today's generation of parents and grandparents either came of age or reared their children. The prevalent images on the television serials of the day such as *Father Knows Best*, *Leave it to Beaver*, and *The Ozzie and Harriet Show* are mythological in their portrayal of the "average happy family." These television situation comedies, extraordinarily popular and powerfully normalizing, appealed to the consensus ideal of the historical family transplanted to the city and suburb: a working dad, a house mom, and the normative heterosexual kids living and adapting, with growing pains and funny problems. Not one out of thousands of these weekly shows ever challenged the fundamental principle that the children of these TV families must be heterosexually identified and presumably would marry, stay married, and have children.

For many families at the time, such cultural images were satisfying and reinforcing—because they guided and mirrored their lives, even if family members were not able to live up to the stereotype in every single respect. But for others, these images were exceedingly painful because they portrayed a family life at odds with their own daily lives and experiences. They represented a pressure to conform—and to keep up with the Joneses in the middle-class. For several million people and their families, these images were—and still remain—hurtful reminders of their "failure" to meet societal expectations, either because they did not have children, or because of divorce or separation, or because of a "family secret."

The Impact of the Myth

The subject of the expectation of grandchildren is particularly central to understanding what is at stake in the Heterosexual Family Myth. Being heterosexual enables people to marry, have children, and eventually enjoy grandchildren. Maybe these events of family life do not bring automatic happiness, as the ideal of heterosexuality implies, but it is pretty certain that having heterosexual children is regarded by most parents as a better formula for happiness than having homosexual children.

It should come as no surprise, therefore, that the first reactions of parents in our study to the discovery that their child was gay or lesbian was, to varying degrees, negative. A few parents in our study even felt traumatized. Some disguised their reactions. But one mother required a psychiatric hospitalization after receiving her son's letter to the family saying that he was gay. Undoubtedly many parents today continue to be disturbed by the news that their child is gay or lesbian—yet by-and-large their reactions are less negative than parents' reactions a generation ago, when, as George Weinberg observed in 1972, the alienation was so great that parents felt their child to be a "member of another species."[1]

When a child tells a parent that she is lesbian or he is gay, the very foundation of the family, the myth of happiness through heterosexual union, is shaken. The telling need not be as traumatic as it was in the case of an eighteen year-old male in our study who could not wait any longer and confessed in desperation on the morning of his sister's wedding. He had for months tried to tell his family. They were in denial and refused to listen. On the wedding day he was of course ignored, and he could no longer bear it. As his parents and sister assembled in the antechamber to the church, with the extended family and a room full of guests waiting in the church, the pressure grew intense, and he blurted out, "I have something to tell you! I am gay!" His parents were furious and his sister and the bridegroom were distraught. One could hardly imagine a worse time to come out—or a more public way to "spill the news." This story, while certainly extreme, illustrates the desperation of gay offspring who feel denied and who then rebel by disclosing their homosexuality at the least opportune time.

As we have learned from our interviews, the moment of disclosure is seen from totally divergent perspectives by the parents and children. Because parents remain invested in upholding the Myth through the life-course of their family, they experience an immediate sense of loss, often coupled with either fear, anger or grief. They have lost an image of who their child was in their eyes and what he or she would become in their fantasy of the future. They cannot imagine how they will cope with this loss. Ironically, their offspring typically experience the moment of disclosure as one of immense gain and relief: of finally claiming freedom to be who they really are. They feel exhilarated by the joy of finally relinquishing the disguises and hidden feelings that had prevented their parents from knowing them.

It is also ironic that the parents may immediately experience the news that their child is homosexual as a repudiation of themselves or their parental role. The parents may feel rejected because they believe their child is distancing or alienating herself from them. Yet, this is the moment when many gay and lesbian offspring may feel closest to their parents and most real. As a recent Israeli study observes, often "gay and lesbian young adults disclose their homosexuality to their parents because they want to get closer to them."[2] When the parent can understand that the disclosure is the child's attempt to be closer, it is highly promising for the integration of the child into the family. The disintegration accelerates when the parent misperceives the disclosure as an act of betrayal.

The disclosure can also make the parents fearful. Growing up with all the negative stereotypes of lesbians or gays, parents often worry about their lesbian or gay child's well-being and are more likely to project a grim future for him or her. Will she live to become the "lonely spinster?" Will he disappear into a dark underworld of furtive encounters? Will their lives be sad and unfulfilling? Will they face discrimination and abuse? As Mary, a sixty-two year-old mother, confessed:

I'm also afraid it will make his life hard. There's the discrimination factor. I'm afraid other people will look down on him. I've heard about homophobic "gay-bashing." What would his neighbors think if they knew? He's active in the community associations—I don't know if they think about it. But what if suddenly they found out they had a couple of homosexuals living there? I don't know. . . . People can be nasty. I've heard of cops stopping gays and beating them up. Life is hard enough at best. I heard about one mother who just kicked her son out. I could never do that. I love him dearly.

Parents also fear for themselves: While gay children may have exited their "closet" by coming out to their parents, the parents suddenly find themselves newly "closeted"—the parents of a gay child. Who can they tell? What will others think of them as parents? Will they be blamed for failing to raise so-called "normal" children, or pitied for being so "afflicted?" Will they be rejected and shunned? Parents may be ashamed to admit these worries to their children, but they were among the most salient concerns articulated to our interviewers.

After a child's disclosure, shame and anger come to be guests of the family for a long time. These smoldering emotions get in the way of family relationships. Anger may spontaneously disrupt discussions and spoil family gatherings. The father or gay son, the mother or lesbian daughter, may later want to reconcile, but they may continue to hold a grudge against the others who are perceived to be rejecting. A moratorium may emerge; the family agrees to a new reign of cold, hard silence. Andrew Boxer has referred to the process as creating a "demilitarized zone" in which both sides agree to suspend conflict by avoiding the topic. The avoidance, however, cannot resolve the problem. The post-disclosure period is not like the formerly secret period before the child came out. The family knows the situation and avoids it, and this becomes a formula for alienation from those they most love. Ultimately, the existence of a demilitarized zone may lead to disintegration of the family. It is as if someone places a sign on the way to a family gathering: "Do not discuss homosexuality or gay and lesbian issues!" As long as this conspiracy of silence reigns, it will not be possible for the parents to find resolution with their lesbian or gay child. Disintegration is inevitable.

After disclosure the parents must make two immediate (and very difficult) steps: they have to deal with giving up their idealizations and expectations, and they have to confront the negative stereotypes attributed to lesbians and gays by the dominant culture. Often, the parents have internalized those negative stereotypes, and it is their own attitudes they must confront. After all, they have been bearers of the dominant culture. Consciously or unconsciously, they have transmitted society's attitudes to their own family.

Parents' difficulty in confronting the cultural myths as they impact on their lesbian and gay children is revealed by Mary, the sixty-two-year-old mother quoted in one of the epigraphs to this chapter:

> It's upsetting to think of sex between Mark and another man. I can't think of him with the opposite sex, either. I can't quite think of sex between two men or two women. . . . But I'm becoming adjusted. He said, "Mother, I'm not going to take you into our bedroom!" Time will heal it though. . . . I just want him to be happy. I try not to think about that part. I mean, we're taught to think that that's not a normal way of life. We think in terms of procreating—that's normal. I said that to my son, and he said, "It is a normal way of life—to me." Well, yes, it's normal to him but it isn't mainstream. But it could be so much worse. I have to be grateful for what I have.

Parents such as Mary have had to cope with a new kind of social experience unknown in history and in our own culture until recently: being the parent of an openly gay- or lesbian-identified child. And they have to negotiate the experience against the stereotypes and without positive rules or norms that might help to guide them toward integration. In the 1960s and 1970s, parents of homosexual offspring were brought into confrontation by the first wave of those who "came out." In the 1980s and 1990s, parents of a second and third wave have had new kinds of concerns to deal with. Among these are the fact that the age of coming out is getting younger and that the risk of contracting AIDS through sexual relations is ever-present in the minds of parents. These waves of parents share the problems and prospects of their children living their entire lives as gay or lesbian in a society that does not honor them and—what is worse—creates many obstacles to homosexual children leading fulfilling and satisfying lives.

Parents often feel that they are alone or even unique in having a gay son or a lesbian daughter. As Amy, a forty-six-year-old mother of three, said about the discovery that her son was gay: "I felt that I was the only one in the world with a gay son." This reaction might surprise the reader. Isn't there so much publicity on television and in the newspapers about these issues today? How could parents not see all the information about anti-homosexual legislation, the military policy of "Don't Ask, Don't Tell," the coming out of "Ellen" in the television program, or the talk show banter about lesbians being good mothers? Yet, the fact is, people can ignore what seems to be irrelevant to their own lives, and they will listen in a totally different way when the news concerns someone they love.

The parents in our study typically didn't think of their children as homosexual prior to the coming-out event. When the occasional parent had suspicions, these were hidden from others, including their spouse. Therefore, the parents had generally responded to media stories with a grain of salt: those stories were removed from their own lives. "That's about somebody else, not me." And many of the parents in their fifties and older came of age in a time when these issues were never discussed in public. "Sex" was private, a dirty subject, and one didn't discuss it with one's parents except under extreme pressure. In fact, the feeling that it is "unnatural" to discuss sexuality permeates many of the stories that parents told about their homosexual children. The surprise that the parents registered on learning of a child's homosexuality also suggests how deeply and well-hidden the secret was in the child. As long as it was hidden, the parents could always feel, "homosexuality was someone else's problem, not ours."

A few parents, however—more typically mothers—have told us that they had long suspected or guessed that their child was gay or lesbian, but they chose to wait for the child to bring it up, or they colluded with the child to keep the secret hidden. In such cases, the shared problem of hiding led to the shared task of how to come out of the closet.

Most parents experience a sort of cognitive dissonance as well.[3] Having been inculcated by the homophobic attitudes of the dominant culture, parents are jarred to find themselves suddenly wondering if these same harsh judgments and painful stereotypes apply to the child they so deeply love and admire.[4] One of the mothers in our study, Flora, captured this feeling when she spoke of the discovery that her son was gay.

> Kevin had dated but it was always a platonic sort of thing. I just thought that he was studious, a late bloomer; that he was interested in his school work. A friend of mine said, "He has plenty of time. It's better that way." Girls liked him very much but he never gave encouragement. . . . All the way along, I kept hoping but I kept wondering in the back of my mind. I wanted a grandchild; I looked forward to him marrying. "What did I do?" I used to ask myself. I asked him if it was a matter of choice and he said "No." He said he'd never been interested in a girl sexually. . . . I wanted a grandchild. Kevin

used to work at a nursery school—he'd take care of forty or forty-five kids. They loved him. I used to think what a wonderful father he'd make.

Flora went on to tell how hard it had been for her to surrender these feelings. Although she was successful in forming a new and more positive relationship with her son, the nostalgia in her story suggests that a part of her still clings to her past image of him.

Virtually all the parents in our study struggled with the inevitable question: Why is my child gay? The very nature of this question derives from negativity, from the way our culture bases its valuation of people on their being heterosexual. If a person is not heterosexual, there must be something wrong, and if there is something wrong, we need only to find its source and fix it. And if we cannot fix it, then we are surely to blame for it. Parents initially can become preoccupied with this issue of blame, of finger-pointing. But laying the "blame" for a child's homosexuality on something or someone is both destructive and inconclusive. In fact, the only "conclusion" that can be arrived at has less to do with the facts of the matter than with what parents believe to be the facts. Most of the parents in our study sought a biological explanation for their child's sexual orientation. Their search for this explanation is an understandable attempt to find a physical cause for a "problem," a means of alleviating the burden of guilt our culture places on parents of lesbians and gay men.

In truth, it is the parents' frame of mind that is most at issue. The child was previously assumed to be straight; none of their other children are lesbian or gay; they are not gay or lesbian themselves; and their society says that somehow they as parents are responsible for this outcome. An explanation in human development or biology is often sought when something is perceived to go wrong.[5] This explains the intense finger-pointing that often surrounds the initial news that the child is gay or lesbian. Who is to blame? If not the father, then the mother; if not her, then a teacher, or sibling, or someone or something else. Yet, as the parents come to accept their child for who he or she is, they come to accept themselves better. The blame game stops.

Children who come out to their family compel parents to reconsider a whole range of attitudes and beliefs. What is right and wrong? How can I go against long-held biases? As Amy, the forty-six-year-old mother, admitted, "None of our friends had gay sons. It took me a long time to tell my mother, because Jay is her only grandson." Amy felt singled out and isolated as a result of learning that her son is gay. For some parents, this is the first time in their lives that they have had to face prejudice or injustice. They certainly have never before felt shame, guilt, and anger regarding the public perception of their own child. This overwhelming sense of uniqueness and isolation, we suggest, stems from the powerful antihomosexual social attitudes of our society. Some parents' ability to understand the plight of their child is finally fostered by the recognition that it is society's homophobia that is isolating them, the parents. The gay or lesbian child was, of course, attempting to cope and master the snake pit of homophobia and hatred in society all along. Paradoxically, only when the parents are able themselves to work through the socially inculcated negative views of homosexuality and to create their own way of acceptance of their child's sexuality can they cease to feel that they have been cast beyond the pale.

2

What Affects
a Family's
Resilience?

As we interviewed the families in our study, we came to discern a path on which they all seemed to embark. Initially, families encountered a period of disintegration characterized at various points by guilt and recrimination, secrecy, impaired relations with others, and shame. Some families moved on to a period of ambivalence involving continued discomfort but with a modicum of hope, often informed by successful disclosure to others. Finally, a number of families entered a state of integration in which the relationships between family members appeared enhanced, the bonds of family and friendship were strengthened, and the families displayed great confidence in themselves and the future. While we will explore these states of experience—disintegration, ambivalence, and integration—in considerable depth in subsequent chapters, we want to consider at this point those factors that seem to affect a family's progress.

Our analysis is shaped in part by the emerging concept of "resilience," i.e., the capacity to emerge from a crisis with greater strength. The renowned family therapist Froma Walsh describes it as "an active process of endurance, self-righting, and growth"[1] that is "forged through adversity, not despite it."[2] Walsh and others have identified a number of important elements that contribute to a family's resilience, including their capacity to empathize with others and engage in social activism,[3] as well as the ability to find meaning, maintain a balance between stability and change, communicate clearly and effectively, and engage in collaborative problem-solving.[4]

In our interviews, we encountered these qualities as well as other aspects of family life that can enhance or inhibit a healthy response. We discovered that certain experiences or conditions in parents' lives seemed to affect their willingness and ability to deal with their child's coming out. For example, some had successfully faced other crises in the past, particularly experiences with illness, addiction, or death. These experiences gave the families a "track record" of sorts. How they responded to previous crises typically predicted how they would deal with this new challenge.

Perhaps the most poignant example is demonstrated in our interview with Phyllis Aaron, the mother of a lesbian daughter who has a chronic and potentially life-threatening disability. (Phyllis also experienced the horror of discovering that one of her children—not her daughter—had been sexually abused by a trusted adult). Phyllis underlined how dealing with her daughter's disability helped temper the pain and sense of failure she felt when her daughter came out: She told us, "My husband and I don't always understand our grief, but we have a warmth and tenderness toward her not afforded our other kids. We both cry a lot. She needs the love she doesn't get from the world." In response to our interview question, "How has learning about your daughter's sexual orientation affected you as an adult and as a parent?" Phyllis responded, "It has instilled in me a pride in my daughter and a recognition of her courage to stand up for who she is—I have a cause to champion and a reason to educate myself to become a more understanding and accepting woman. I am enriched."

The Aarons, by virtue of their past experiences with the crises of their daughter's disability and of another child's victimization, have learned to distinguish the desire to protect from the desire to love. Echoing what perhaps every parent of a child harmed or disabled must eventually learn, Phyllis commented, "I need to be aware of why and what I do for my daughter so I don't overdo or overprotect. She doesn't need my protection–she needs my love." The Aarons have learned to find meaning in the challenge of difference. They were prepared to deal with this new difference, their daughter's sexual orientation, by applying the lessons learned from one crisis to the challenges of another. We believe that families who have faced serious challenges of this kind in their past are, ironically, equipped to deal better with the challenge of their child's coming out.

Our findings suggest that whether or not parents were divorced also made a difference in the their capacity to adjust to having a gay child. Approximately 29 percent of the parents we placed in both the "Ambivalent" and "Disintegrated" categories were divorced. One mother told us that she and her husband separated shortly after she learned that both of her sons were gay. "If there's a weakness in the marriage," she remarked, "it can break its back!"

Regardless of their marital status, however, it mattered that the parents communicated, cooperated, and remained cohesive during the process of the child's coming out. Those who maintained some sort of sound parental partnership even when separated or divorced seemed to adjust well to the knowledge that their child was gay or lesbian. For example, Kathy O'Donnell, the divorced mother of a gay son, Jonathan, told us that she and her ex-husband, Andrew, had worked out a comfortable joint custody arrangement and remained conveniently located in proximity to each other to minimize the disruption to their children's lives. Notable throughout our interview with her was an absence of hostility or resentment toward her ex-husband. She described how her ex-husband provided some experiences to her teenage children that she could not. "The children all travel with their father, who is a compulsive traveler and takes them on lots of nice trips, which is lovely for them since I can't afford to be doing that." She also described Andrew as "a very loving father who cares profoundly for his children." We look more closely at the O'Donnell family in chapter 6, but suffice it to say at this point that Jonathan's coming out served as a catalyst for immense positive change. The respectful relationship the parents maintained with each other despite their divorce allowed the integrative process to proceed unimpeded. Divorce is, clearly, not in itself a barrier to the healthy integration some families achieve.

Some of the parents we interviewed seemed to use other experiences of being "different" to help them understand the importance of tolerating "difference" and to facilitate integration. Alicia Dawson, an African-American mother of a lesbian daughter, told of the conflicts with her daughter she had had over her daughter's "negative attitude and aggression toward men." She declared, "I taught my children to let people be what they are. I resent general hate!" One might reasonably speculate that Alicia's own experiences with the effects of racism have sensitized her to displays of such "general hate" in others, including her own daughter. It should be no surprise, therefore, that Alicia regards herself as "an activist for human rights" through her involvement in PFLAG. Furthermore, despite the significant differences between mother and daughter, their relationship is clearly within the "Integrated" category.

Several of the parents we interviewed had some previous exposure to lesbian or gay people, which greatly affected their initial responses to learning their child was homosexual. Perhaps the most striking example was John Billings, a law enforcement officer and the father of a lesbian daughter. At the time that his daughter came out to him, he recalled, "I was assigned to the gay squad and I had to arrest gays when they put a hand on us to make sexual advances." John ascribed his initial negative response to his daughter's disclosure to this fact: "I was arresting people for that, and here my daughter was one!" John's strong association of homosexuality with criminality made his adjustment very difficult. He was able to tell only one person outside of the family. He admitted having felt "like a failure" as a parent because of his daughter's sexual orientation. Interestingly, however, after his daughter's disclosure, John found he would sometimes choose not to arrest people as part of his job and eventually arranged to be transferred to a new position outside of the "gay squad." However gradual, John's love for his daughter instigated a change in his view of the homosexual.

Upon learning that his daughter was a lesbian, another father whom we interviewed confided in a lesbian friend of his at his workplace. The support and openness of this friend went a long way toward reassuring him that he could cope with his lesbian daughter's disclosure and accept her. By learning especially that others, such as the parents of his friend, could accept having a homosexual child, his own path to love and openness was made easier.

Kathy O'Donnell, the divorced mother described earlier, had also had positive experiences with gay men through her work in a retail store: "That was my first real contact with gay men as groups, blatantly gay, without any need to be ashamed or hide it, and rightfully so. When we moved to this house, I had a friend, a young gay man, just a love, and he helped me move here."

Kathy noted that after her son came out, this friend (who subsequently moved abroad) and her gay son developed a helpful and supportive correspondence.

In the Jeffers family, the father and mother had both experienced very different interactions with gay people. Marcia Jeffers explained:

> My husband used to live in San Francisco after high school. He lived close to gay bathhouses and I think he formed negative impressions because of the explicit sexual nature of the bathhouses. He found it repugnant. It was Castro Street that he lived on. I think that he thought that our son's being gay meant he therefore would be promiscuous and spend time at gay bathhouses, bars, and pick up people in public toilets, etc. He just thought that was part of being gay. He thought there would be lots of casual sexual contacts. Well,

as it's turned out, our son hasn't behaved that way—and my husband is reassured. He understands more. He doesn't reject that aspect of our son.

Marcia's own experience better prepared her for the news of her son's sexual orientation:

My best friend from high school is a lesbian, so I had a positive impression of at least lesbians. She was my best friend in high school; we started sixth grade together. I was at their house lots. Her mom called me their "other daughter." I was really a part of the family. . . . I knew nothing was wrong in the family to cause homosexuality. There was no dominant or submissive mother or father. She had articulate and assertive parents. They were close—she wasn't rejected, nor was she overly fussed about. . . . So whatever I might have thought, impressions I got from society, didn't fit.

As a result of this experience, Marica was less likely to blame herself and felt more at ease with her son's sexual orientation. In the context of the silence or condemnation that usually greets the topic of homosexuality in American culture, together with the relative invisibility of lesbians and gay men until recently, these limited experiences become quite powerful. If one lacks personal contact with gays and lesbians, the more negative stereotypes that are rampant in society often constitute one's sole notion of gays or lesbians. Those stereotypes can trigger the same fear and anxiety in parents as they do in society at large. Parents' reactions to their gay or lesbian children may be unduly shaped by the stereotypes that are part and parcel of our culture. But through the increased visibility of lesbians and gay men, parents can hope to learn more fully about their homosexual offspring's life. Only when large numbers of gays and lesbians come out can parents and society in general begin to discover the range of "normal people" like their own child who are attracted to persons of the same sex. This is one of the many powerful arguments for coming out.

In our study we looked at a number of other key factors that we thought might affect a family's capacity to integrate their gay or lesbian child into their lives. These included the age of the child and of the parents at the time the child came out, the religiosity of the family, the parents' education, the relationship between a parent's first reactions and subsequent adjustment, and the gender of the parent and the child. We will examine each of these in turn.

The parents we interviewed are typically more open than others. It is important to acknowledge this point because the group we surveyed is not representative of all parents of gay or lesbian offspring. As we said earlier, many of the parents we interviewed were recruited through PFLAG in Chicago and through the Gay and Lesbian Youth Program at Horizons Community Services (the gay and lesbian social services agency in Chicago). Consequently, we knew we were likely to obtain a sample skewed toward the more integrated end of the continuum. Nevertheless, the interviews are richly detailed accounts of the experiences of these families, positive and negative. We are able to discern from them some very significant factors that characterize and differentiate experiences, and these have general implications for all families.

Certain factors seemed to have little or no bearing on the family's capacity to achieve a high level of integration. The average age of the child at the point of coming out to parents was 21.2 years old, with ages ranging from fifteen to thirty years old. The average age of the child's mother and father at the point of coming out was 49.3 years old and 51.9 years old respectively, with mothers ranging in age from thirty-seven to sixty-seven and fathers ranging in age from thirty-five to sixty-eight (three fathers were deceased in our survey). Neither the age of the child nor of the parents at the point of coming out seemed to have significant effect on the family's capacity to integrate the gay or lesbian child.

Similarly, in our study it did not seem to matter how religious the parents were. While other studies point to the role of religiosity in family attitudes, we speculate that this is changing in society (though we must acknowledge that fundamentalists were underrepresented in our samples).[5] In any case, there was no significant correlation between how often our parents attended religious services or how important they regarded their religion to be and their response to their gay or lesbian child. The "Disintegrated" families were only slightly more religious than the "Integrated" families.

It did appear, however, that parents in the "Integrated" group had generally achieved higher levels of education than those in the other two categories. They were more likely to have completed college, and 54 percent of the "Integrated" group had also completed advanced degrees compared to 39 percent of the "Ambivalent" group and none of the "Disintegrated" group.

We also found that parents who were more supportive at the time of their gay or lesbian child's disclosure were more likely to achieve high levels of integration than those who were less supportive at the initial point. Parents in the "Integrated" group were also less likely to have suspected their child was gay prior to the disclosure. Somehow these parents were better able to respond to the news even though they had no idea it was coming, a trend illustrated in table 1 (see appendix 1). We suspect that at least some of this capacity to respond positively derives from a history of crisis and coping, which had produced a pattern of constructive response.

But why should parents who had previous suspicions of their child's homosexuality generally have a more troubled response? Perhaps those parents who had indeed suspected their child was gay or lesbian had been resisting an actual acknowledgement for some time. The disclosure, therefore, confirmed the worst fear of such parents and/or violated an implicit agreement to deny or conceal the obvious. Their response might thus have been more of an attempt to reinstate secrecy— to deny and conceal again, accompanied by a deep sense of hurt and betrayal when this failed. Here we see one of the many sources of disintegration—a failure to deal with the reality that the child is gay.

The one aspect of parental reaction that mattered greatly was the gender of the child. Our study confirmed what previous studies have also found: families are better able to integrate gay sons than lesbian daughters. Table 2 (see appendix 1) illustrates this phenomenon by showing the percentages in our study of each type of family with gay sons or lesbian daughters. Approximately 82 percent of the families in the integration phase had gay sons, compared to only 57 percent of those in the disintegration phase. More starkly, only 18.2 percent of the integrated families had lesbian daughters compared to 42.9 percent of the disintegrated families. It is hard to know how typical these results are, but our study, and stories in the culture, imply a general pattern.

Everyone knows, of course, that traditionally men and women have different roles in our society. Also the status, resources, and power of the genders are not equal, as illustrated by the fact that men and women in the same positions in the same job often have different salary levels, with women typically making less money than men. Perhaps a possible explanation of the greater perceived difficulty of integrating a lesbian daughter into the family has to do with the gender role expectations our culture places on men and women. Men are valued for their capacity to work, provide, compete, achieve, and succeed. Male status is thus based on such personality attributes as independence, work and income, self-reliance and individualism. By contrast, our traditional culture values women for their roles as mothers and moral guardians, emphasizing the ability to nurture and love, have children and take care of them, and subordinate their feelings and needs if necessary to keep relationships together and provide a safe, warm place for family.[6] Of course these are cultural ideals. Many men and women do not fit into them and have different aspirations. In fact, it is well known that the nature of our economy today generally requires a two-income family, with both women and men working outside the home and thus making their lives ever more complex. Nonetheless, these economic changes have not yet altered the cultural ideals of gender roles, especially for women.

Families may more readily integrate the gay son because he can still fulfill the key role expectations of being male in spite of his homosexuality. He can succeed at a career, achieve status through higher income, and gain respect for being self-reliant and becoming a separate individual. Those same achievements by a lesbian daughter, however, conflict with the family's role expectations for females. They typically desire to see her marry and have children. She may not get the family recognition she deserves for having a successful career. The older she gets, the more she may be disparaged for not being married and for lacking the affiliative status of a husband who is established and successful in the community. Because she does not enter into a heterosexual marriage, she will never have children sanctified by church and/or society in the traditional way. (It should be noted, of course, that lesbians and gay men are increasingly choosing to have children by means of surrogate pregnancy, donor insemination, or adoption). Since she does not have a husband and children from a man, her feminine status is always compromised. Thus, she remains a kind of outlaw to her own gender, for it is assumed that she cannot serve as the maker and guardian of the family like her own mother.

While stereotypes are changing and in some quarters are no longer salient, we found that many mothers and fathers still react in horror to the announcement of their lesbian daughter's sexual orientation. But it is fathers that seem most resentful of their lesbian daughters. Perhaps that resentment is often related to the feeling that their daughters have "rejected them" by refusing to have a husband and heterosexual marriage. Both mothers and fathers also feel that their lesbian daughter will never serve the function of keeping the family together and fulfilling the more traditional role of producing grandchildren.

Indeed, the fear that the daughter will never provide the grandchildren that parents need in order to achieve their own feeling of having succeeded as parents is profound. We have reviewed this point previously but need to stress here what this anxiety does to thwart the integration of the lesbian daughter into the family. Most parents feel a deep sense of fulfillment when they are presented with grandchildren. They feel deeply affirmed that the sacrifices and choices they made in their lives are now valued, even emulated, by their children. Grandparenthood also bestows on the grandparents generativity: the opportunity to enter into a new role with a grandchild—to be a source of wisdom, history, and connection to one's ancestry. As any doting grandparent will tell you, toward their grandchildren they can feel unconditional love. The birth of grandchildren therefore constitutes a major milestone, if not a capstone, to a life of labor and sacrifice. Thus it is no surprise that almost all of the parents we interviewed harbored strong feelings about the issue of grandchildren. Many felt deeply disappointed by this loss, especially if they were parents of daughters. Because the lesbian daughter does not emulate the life of her mother in the most culturally and personally significant way—bearing and raising children in a heterosexual marriage—it simply becomes more difficult for some parents to take pride in a lesbian daughter, as they might in a gay son. No doubt as the number of lesbian mothers grows this reaction will change.[7] Some day all of these changes may create a wider range of appreciation of the daughter's achievements other than motherhood.

Ann Muller (herself the mother of a gay son) believes that because lesbians are more likely than gay men to enter into heterosexual relationships episodically, parents may long continue to hope that their lesbian daughter will "change." They may also regard their daughter's same-sex orientation as a "phase." In the past daughters may have themselves reinforced this hope of change by initially defining themselves as bisexual. Even today younger lesbians have more experiences with the opposite sex due to gender role pressures on females to date and marry.[8] The family, therefore, may continue to hope and to resist making the necessary accommodations for integrating the lesbian identity of their daughter. Gay sons, on the other hand, tend to remain unequivocally gay: to consistently define themselves as gay and relate romantically only to other men. The family grows more certain about their son's sexual orientation, therefore, and its reactions are less ambiguous, more final.

Parents also tend to think of a gay son's homosexuality as having been caused by a "biological force," whereas they are more conflicted about the origins of a daughter's homosexuality. Some parents think their lesbian offspring have "chosen" a different "lifestyle." Therefore, they may blame daughters more than sons. Fathers in particular encounter more difficulty accepting a daughter's lesbian identity. Ann Muller reported from her study that the mothers of lesbians complained of hurt and loss, while the fathers were more likely to express anger and to break off ties. There are thus many disrupted father/daughter bonds in families with lesbian daughters.

Additionally, we found that a family with a lesbian daughter was less likely to achieve a high level of integration if she was their only daughter. This suggests that having a lesbian daughter was less disruptive to the family if another daughter was present who could fulfill the more traditional role expectations for daughters.

As the following chapters will illustrate, parents who want to integrate their gay sons or lesbian daughters into their families openly are compelled to deal with societal attitudes and beliefs about homosexuality in a whole new way. They must struggle to cope effectively with a range of feelings brought about by profound social forces. They are constrained to battle the cultural image of the heterosexual family, the constructed mythology left over from our past, the cultural survivals of the Golden Age of *Father Knows Best*. The pressure imposed by the heterosexist "Myth" encourages the family to continue to hide "family secrets," to pretend that everything is "normal," while discord and unhappiness are building and the family risks the disruption and even the loss of precious ties. Integrated families face these challenges too, but they also manage to undergo a process of change that enables them to see past the stereotypes and create a new image of the family, based upon the reality that their child is lesbian or gay. They have lost a myth but they have grown into a better family. That is the lesson of the stories that follow.

3

When a Family Loses Its Way

Disintegration

When he came out, we told [our son] Rick that we didn't understand; that we were hurt and disappointed, but that we accepted him and we were sure we would come to terms with it. Those were the things we said in his presence. But behind his back, we were in a state of hysteria. I really think I went into the closest thing to a nervous breakdown I've ever experienced. I was hating Rick for what he was doing to himself and to the family. I felt humiliation—what if others find out, such as members of the family! I thought he was destroying our entire family.

—*Betty Stein, sixty-one -year-old mother of a gay son*

BETTY EXPRESSED A COMMON REACTION to a child's initial disclosure that he is gay. She feared he would destroy the family—a family she had regarded as perfectly normal and stable until now. Yet, to a considerable extent, her son's disclosure revealed a previously hidden breach in the family and offered that family an opportunity to mend it. That hidden breach lay in the pain and alienation of her son who concealed a core aspect of his personality from his parents for several years.

The illusion of the Stein family as "perfect" was obtained only through this concealment. What appeared integrated rested on a state of fragmentation—the son was only partly known to his family. He had felt constrained in all of his interactions with them to pretend to preserve and support the cultural ideal of heterosexuality.

As we have been suggesting, families seem to fall into three broad categories of response and organization after a gay or lesbian child's disclosure: Disintegration, Ambivalence, or Integration. The chapters to follow will describe and profile families in each of these categories or stages. But first we will describe in some detail the factors involved in these designations. In our study we identified fourteen separate criteria that reflect growth and change (see appendix 2). We used these criteria to assess levels of integration within a family (which can, of course, change as the family learns to become more accepting). We then classified those levels into the following six categories of change.

Overcoming Shame

The first category relates to the degree to which families have overcome shame. Most parents seem to experience profound shame when they learn that their offspring is gay or lesbian. They express that shame perhaps as a fear of being diminished in the eyes of others, or a sense of having failed as a parent. Conversely, they may seek to blame others—the school, the culture, or, in the case of some parents, each other. The conflict is destructive, and the resentment such feelings breed is stifling. Shame is a disintegrating force.

Families who are in the ambivalent phase struggle more internally with the sense of shame. Their public behavior may suggest tolerance and acceptance of their gay child, but feelings of embarrassment or shame persist quietly within.

Families that have achieved integration experience more congruence between their public behavior and their private thoughts. They blame no one because they see nothing bad or wrong. There are no recriminations or accusations; no one is uttering, "You should have paid more attention to him!" or "You shouldn't have doted on her!" The gay aspect of their child's identity is genuinely thought to be unique and at least of some value, if not "a gift."

The Family's Disclosure to Others

A second dimension by which we assessed the quality of integration involved the extent to which families disclosed the child's sexual orientation to others. In correlating this dimension with "integration," we assumed that those families with a greater level of shame, discomfort, or embarrassment about the matter will be less likely to disclose to others. Non-disclosure, especially to close relatives, friends, or colleagues, may necessitate varying levels of deception or obfuscation that preclude successful integration. For example, the lesbian daughter may "know" not to bring her partner with her to an event involving the extended family, because "it will raise too many questions."

Impact on Family Relations

The third category involves self-reported changes in family relationships. Here we found that the more integrated families reported some positive change in either the marital relationship, the parents' relationships with their gay or lesbian offspring, or the general level of family functioning. The latter may include improved communication among members of the family, or a change in the role that members play in the family that enhances their ability to respond to problems. For example, the gay son who becomes more confident and assertive in the family may even begin to function as a role model for a younger sibling; or a nonexpressive father may become more forthcoming and loving in the marital relationship. We observed, of course, that some of the families who displayed the most progress toward integration did not report much change in family relationships because these relationships were already quite good.

Appreciation of Child's Sexual Orientation

Another category that indicated growth and change to us was suggested by the degree to which parents acknowledged an appreciation of the gay or lesbian offspring's sexual orientation. In our interviews with parents, this sometimes took the form of commenting positively on the increased maturity, happiness, or contentment of the child, or respect or pride in the child's manner of handling the coming out process. Some parents also noted the positive contribution that the child's disclosure made to their own lives.

We do recognize, however, that families in some cultural communities achieve a certain level of integration without explicit disclosure or discussion within the family. In the Asian-American community, for example, there may be no equivalent word or concept for a "gay" identity, and yet the Asian family, by virtue of strong familial loyalty, may make great efforts to integrate this aspect of a child's life into ongoing relationships. In other cases, it is as if a rule of quid pro quo applies: if the gay or lesbian child agrees not to discuss the matter explicitly, the parents will agree to accommodate to key aspects of the child's life.

Inclusion

This dimension, which we call inclusion, constitutes an additional category of change we sought to assess in determining a family's progress toward integration. We noted that, whereas some families could not imagine incorporating their son's or daughter's lover into family events, others not only did so but even became quite friendly with the entire "in-law" constellation. This may seem startling to some, yet we saw numerous examples of this change. More important, the new family constellation became a web of genuine support to all.

Community Involvement

Another indicator that we used to assess levels of integration in a family concerned the parent's involvement with nonfamily lesbians and gay men or their parents. Families that appeared the most integrated felt their experience had been significantly affirmed or "normalized" by such contacts. Some had joined the organization Parents, Families, and Friends of Lesbians and Gays (PFLAG). Some became acquainted with the gay or lesbian friends of their children. Others volunteered to work in service organizations within the gay or lesbian community. Many parents cited these experiences as contributing significantly to their own sense of well-being and accomplishment.

Future Time

Finally, we looked at the degree to which parents could project major life events for their gay or lesbian offspring over the lifespan. We established this criterion because of the evidence that parents might initially have difficulty envisioning a gay or lesbian child's future, and it is critical that families be able to envision milestones in the lives of their children in order to progress toward shared goals and to feel confident about their children's future.[1] The challenge, of course, is that parents, like their gay and lesbian children, are bereft of role models and examples of what these milestones might be. The silence and condemnation surrounding homosexuality in our society leaves a disturbing void. Lacking accurate and in-depth information, families and their gay or lesbian children are left to fill the gap only with false myths or negative stereotypes. For example, parents may assume that being gay or lesbian means growing old in a context of isolation and bitterness, working only in stereotypical "gay" careers, or (for males especially) seeking sex furtively and promiscuously. Younger gay males, witnessing the numbers of gay men in their forties succumbing to AIDS, may conclude that the deadly virus is all that awaits them, and they despair.

They do not know or see the countless men beyond middle age who lead vital, contented lives, both as individuals and as couples. Nor do young lesbians or gay men always see the extensive social and friendship networks in which so many of their older counterparts thrive. Parents lack such information as well. They are familiar only with the milestones we associate with a heterosexual lifecourse: first dates, engagement, wedding, child-rearing, career advancement, second careers, grandchildren, retirement, and so forth. With no clear compass by which to gauge a life trajectory for lesbians and gay men, parents cannot function fully as "guides" for their gay children, nor can they adequately provide the support and reassurance that young adults so desperately require as they advance into full adulthood. In contrast, when both parent and child are accurately informed, the more desirable and traditional problem-solving alliances upon which parents and children rely can function effectively.

The following table summarizes these contrasts between Disintegration, Ambivalence, and Integration.

Table 1 Summary of How Families Differ

	Disintegration	*Ambivalence*	*Integration*
Expressions of shame or guilt	Considerable guilt; sense of embarrassment or failure	Mixed; internal reaction more shame-based than what is presented publicly	Little if any shame or recrimination; public appreciation congruent with internal reactions
The family's disclosure to others	Limited; "Don't ask, don't tell," fears of damaging others or destroying relationships. Few if any disclosures outside of family	Ambivalence about the need to tell versus the discomfort of telling; some extended family or friends have been told	Secrecy regarded as a burden; costs of being "closeted" acknowledged; most family and friends have been told
Impact on relationships in the family	Same or greater degrees of distance or conflict than prior to disclosure	Positive change in some relationships; increased communication but lack of resolution	Sense of enhancement in relationships; conflicts generate closeness rather than distance
Appreciation of sexual orientation of offspring	None	Acknowledgment of incresed understanding; sensitivity	Able to identify unique positive contribution of gay or lesbian offspring
Involvement with gay/lesbian community or parents of lesbians or "in-laws"	Little or no contact	Contact may be with parents of gays, but rarely with lesbians or gay men	Often report involvement with PFLAG; contact with lesbians or gay men who may or not be friends of gay offspring

Table 1 *(continued)*

	Disintegration	Ambivalence	Integration
Inclusion of friends, lovers of gay offspring or "in-laws"	Little or no contact	Variable. Conflict within family about including lover	Marked inclusion; contact which, if not frequent, is usually positive
Ability to pro- ject a future for lesbian or gay offspring	Rarely	More able to do so; sense of uncertainity or fear	Generally able to project positive events for at least next 10 years

Disintegration

To the extent that gay or lesbian offspring have overcome within themselves the effects of the stigma associated with homosexuality, the disclosure to family may represent an act of love and healing. The child is acting in a state of integrity and is therefore taking a courageous step. It is as if he or she is saying: "I am no longer ashamed. Rather, I am worthy of the love of my family and will lay claim to it now by disclosing to them who I really am. As I love them, so I invite them to love me."

As we noted earlier, some parents reported in our interviews that they had a notion that their child was gay or lesbian even before disclosure. Often, those parents performed their own dance of denial in the hope that the child's homosexuality could disappear. The creation of a "demilitarized zone" of avoidance was not uncommon. For some, it brought about pseudo-intimacy in the family, along with a sense of desperation conditioned by an agreement to ignore the unmentionable. For others, this denial created a set of rigid alliances in the family wherein anger and fear were displaced in order to avoid disclosure of the massive secret. The fact that some parents truly had no idea that their child was gay or lesbian testifies, sadly, to the child's uncanny ability to fragment his or her life and conceal its parts.

The child who voluntarily discloses his or her sexual orientation is challenging a powerful family secret that up to now has maintained itself by fragmentation. Fragmentation is by definition a fragile system. The child's disclosure has immense power, for in that very moment of revelation, the weakness of the system is revealed. The disclosure causes people to feel naked and vulnerable. That vulnerability is an aspect of the phase we call Disintegration that most families with a gay or lesbian child must move through—and, it is to be hoped, will learn from. Though many families move out of the Disintegration phase, others, unfortunately, do not. In the latter case, the child's pursuit of a healthy and integrated life is substantially thwarted.

The Disintegrating Effects of Shame

In order for a cultural ideal to survive, deviation from that ideal must be stigmatized, i.e., branded as disgraceful. There are numerous examples of this in our daily lives. The cultural ideal of "work," for example, is a powerful force in modern American society. We call it the "work ethic" and view someone who does not work as "weak" or "undeserving." Unemployment or underemployment is stigmatized and, of course, that stigma is internalized by those who are unemployed or underemployed. In periods of high unemployment, it is no surprise that the incidence of depression and suicide rises due, in large part, to the shame of being out of work, even when the unemployment is a product of events the individual could never be expected to control, e.g., a plant closing, or a major recession or depression.

Similarly, the cultural ideal of heterosexual marriage and parenting is reinforced by the shaming of those who do not conform. That shame is just as toxic in its effects on lesbians, gay men, and their families as the shame of unemployment is on the unemployed. Shame is even far more powerful than simple guilt—a word we all too easily associate with shame. Guilt is a feeling of remorse for having done something wrong. It is best addressed through acknowledgement of wrongdoing and an effort to correct its effects, to make amends. Shame, on the other hand, involves a profound negation or devaluing of oneself—by society and by the self that has internalized society's values. The shamed individual feels, "I am bad, a failure, worthless, wholly without meaning or value." No acknowledgement of wrongdoing can heal a soul of shame; acknowledgement can only reinforce the sense of unworthiness. To be ashamed is to be exiled—as cast out from the community as Adam and Eve were from the Garden of Eden. The fall from grace is so painful and heartrending that it is no wonder gay and lesbian offspring go to such great lengths at times to protect their parents and themselves from shame and social rejection.

Sometimes members of the family blame themselves for a child's homosexuality. This internalization of blame produces the feelings of guilt so many parents initially experience when they discover that their child is lesbian or gay. In an effort to manage guilt, sometimes parents resort to blaming others or each other. They mistakenly believe that if they can just assign blame or expurgate guilt, all will be well.

Unfortunately, when the source of such guilt is the intense shame associated with homosexuality in our culture, the guilt cannot be so easily resolved. It becomes a "complicated guilt,"—that is, complicated by the shame with which it is infused. By contrast, "simple guilt" is more easily resolved. For example, if we feel guilty for not inviting a friend to a party, we can apologize, make amends, and attempt to restore a damaged friendship. But when parents learn their child is gay or lesbian, the shame-based nature of guilt and blame complicates the picture immeasurably, so that no apology or amends can alleviate the pain, much less restore relationships. Rather, the parents and child must reach a totally new understanding of life and love—a complex task not so easily accomplished. Yet only such a new understanding can provide a real antidote to shame.

The Spauldings—Disintegration Takes Hold

Shame is the central issue in those families we viewed as being disintegrated. Its effects are manifest in nearly every thought, action, and decision the family makes in response to learning their child is lesbian or gay. The Spauldings represent a family in just such a distressed state. Hank and Margot Spaulding are a lower-middle-class working couple in the suburbs of Chicago. When we first interviewed them, Hank was forty-six years old and Margot was forty-one. They had been married for twenty-two years. They had a daughter, who lived on the east coast, and a son, Jamie, who was twenty and who had recently come out as gay. The parents had a binational marriage: Hank was American and Margot from Southern Europe, where they met when Hank was in the service.

Jamie started going to the Horizons youth group at the end of his high school years. It was not long afterward that Margot found out that he was gay. The family's reaction was immediately negative, though the depth of their feelings came out only with the passing weeks and months. Jamie and his father had always had a rocky relationship. After

Jamie's sexual orientation was discovered, the family disintegrated significantly. When we first spoke with Margot Spaulding, she conveyed the deep anger and frustration with Jamie that she had felt over many years. The cause of her feeling was not his sexuality, though that became part of it; rather, it had more to do with his personality and her conviction that they had long been at odds. The degree of her emotion was remarkable in the initial interview, because two years had already passed since she learned of her son's homosexuality. So much negative feeling, so long after the triggering events, already marked this family as atypical compared to other parents we interviewed. The Spauldings's extraordinarily negative response was illustrated by Margot's remark in the initial interview that she wished Jamie had "remained in denial," and her lament, "When finally I had to face facts, I wanted to kill myself. I went from anger, to pity, to wanting to kill myself again. It hurt so much."

Margot admitted that she felt that Jamie was "different" from the start, when he was born. But she did not immediately label the difference as "homosexual":

I already knew it when he was about six years old. I would think, "If I didn't know better, I would say [that he is gay]." . . . But I thought it could not happen to me!—That only happens to other people [laugh]! As he grew older, he had a lot of difficulty in school. On Halloween when he was in sixth or seventh grade, some kids smeared "little gay boy" on the garage. I wiped it off before he saw it.

During the course of the interview, she reiterated her shock and despair at finding out that Jamie was gay:

There is a plan to things—cradle to grave. I'm very methodological. I have all my life planned out. Everything has its place. He interrupted my little boxes. I had been gradually, for fifteen years, finding out. I had battled with him from kindergarten through graduation. It had been one battle after another . . . and now I thought, "What can I do? What's left for me to do?" I felt helpless because there's nothing I can do about this, I would be fighting his nature. I felt defeated.

Margot had some perspective about her feelings, but it did not alleviate her despair: "When you hear programs of things on television, a mother with two sons, one of them gay—I thought that it was nice that they can admit it so openly and were coping; no,—not coping, they had accepted it! I thought to myself, I could never do that!"

Margot's ambivalence was palpable. She often expressed affection toward Jamie and wanted him to be close, but at other times she resented his dependence and especially the new burdens imposed upon her by having to deal with his homosexuality.

Jamie and his father had seldom been close, and their relationship worsened over the years. Jamie's disclosure aggravated Hank's antipathy toward his son, as if Hank was trying to manage his shame for having a gay son by blaming and shaming the son. Margot reported:

> His father used to put Jamie down. When the three of us were together, I would always sit there . . . and wonder what would come out of [Hank's] mouth next! I would always take Jamie's side. . . . I do have to protect Jamie. My husband doesn't need protection. As of last summer, he was always wanting me to choose him over Jamie. He didn't want Jamie around, he would much rather have seen him dead. I told him, "No." But then we had it out last summer. I had to choose between him and Jamie. I told him he'd better pack his bags. He will never accept Jamie being gay.

Through words such as these we came to understand that not only was Jamie's relationship with his father and his mother very troubled but also their own relationship had gotten very tangled up in the issue of Jamie's homosexuality. The marriage deteriorated. Margot often resorted to cynicism and irony about the situation, while Hank engaged in outright put-downs, abusive language, and threats directed toward his son and, sometimes, by innuendo, to Jamie's protector, Margot.

Her account of Hank's behavior was tinged with her anger and sorrow. "I told my husband the only thing I expect of him is to leave Jamie alone. I let him know, 'I'm tired of your stupid remarks about Jamie that you say to him, or that you say when he's not around,' " she recalled in the first interview. "Once Hank knew Jamie was gay, when he admitted it to himself last summer, when he couldn't fool himself anymore, he had to face the fact. Then he started making negative comments, dropping snotty remarks here, there, and everywhere." One day Jamie brought some of his gay friends home. His father threw a fit, and the boys had to leave the house. Margot noted, "After that Hank was snotty for three or four weeks and finally we had the big fight." She warned her husband to stop the abusive behavior or it would force her to leave him or end the marriage. Thus things continued for months.

Then Jamie went away to college. But the events of the past months left a bad and tense feeling in the home—there was only separation, not resolution. Margot remarked, "It didn't stop until we went to see Jamie at school. But for a couple, three months, we were close to a divorce. I did not want to sit between two chairs and be confronted with his and Jamie's stupid remarks because Jamie would come right back with something stupid."

Instead of a direct confrontation, father and son exchanged snide remarks, which Margot saw as cowardly: "Neither one was man enough to stand up for what he thinks and talk about it. I guess they have—what is the word?—a truce." A demilitarized zone had been established—a frequent pattern in disintegrated families that fail to communicate and lose their dignity and their respect for each other.

Margot remembered the "truce" and where it left the family:

Now we don't talk about [Jamie being gay] anymore. When Jamie was home for Christmas, we went out to dinner, we talked about school, we totally ignored the fact that Jamie is gay. [Jamie and his father] tolerate each other but that's all. They never really had a relationship. . . . But his father doesn't want him around anymore. I told him, "Don't push me into taking sides." . . . His relationship with Mona, our daughter, is very different. He used to spend lots of time with her. He got along better with the girl than the boy. He likes girls. . . . But with Jamie it is different. They have no relationship.

During the time of the initial interview, Mona and Jamie were close and they enjoyed each other's company and support. These alliances of some family members in the face of conflict may provide the only thing a gay or lesbian child can hang on to at times. Although Jamie and Mona were able to create an adult and genuinely integrated relationship, as sister and brother, their parents were in a very different state.

Margot talked in the initial interview of the efforts of the family at the beginning to seek help from outside. They went to a psychologist briefly. "My husband said Jamie would wind up like Rock Hudson. Dead." Soon the therapy was aborted, as Hank refused to go back.

Margot felt that whatever change developed after Jamie came out was all negative and continued to deteriorate. One evening, when

Jamie was home for the weekend, he and Hank got into "a bad fight." Her husband had had too much to drink, Margot said. Now they became confrontational: "They screamed and shouted at each other, about Jamie's being gay. He said that he would rather see Jamie dead. I told Jamie to shut up. But I'll defend my child against anyone." After that fight, communication between the parents and their child skidded even lower.

As she talked of this change, Margot was clear that Jamie's coming out affected the relationship she had with her husband negatively. She told us that she could see nothing positive about Jamie's being gay. As an afterthought, she commented: "At least now I don't have to guess anymore." She worried that Jamie was not taking suitable precautions against AIDS. She said that she spoke in a caring way to Jamie and he reassured her that he did take precautions.

The resentment between Jamie and his father would not heal. As the years went by, and Jamie graduated from college, he returned to Chicago and got a job. Though there was no closeness between them, father and son tolerated each other. However, on occasion the family would blow up, and the cycle would start again. Jamie's parents would not accept his gay friends or the man who eventually became his lover.

As a postscript, we were able to do several subsequent interviews with the Spauldings almost a decade later. We found that the family had calmed down and, gradually, the truce struck between father and son had congealed into a permanent silence. Occasionally, sarcasm or ridicule would erupt, but there were no longer open fights. All the years he was with his partner in Chicago, Jamie's parents never once visited their home nor invited Jamie's partner to their home. Holidays necessitated splitting. At first Jamie accepted this, but gradually he came to despise it. When Jamie's partner became ill and eventually died from AIDS, his sister gave staunch support throughout the hard times. But Jamie kept the crisis hidden from his parents, and he did not reach out to them for support even at the time of his lover's death and his own grief. The bitterness this created has still not left. When Jamie's father died soon after, following a brief illness, his mother, alone for the first time in her life, became increasingly demanding. First her daughter and then her son were alienated from her. The family could not seem to support each other in grief. Today, the Spaulding family, without Hank, remains disjointed, and the sense of fragmentation communicated so strongly by

Margot in the initial interview has continued over the years, without reconciliation.

The Spauldings managed shame by blaming each other. From the beginning Hank demeaned Jamie for failing to live up to his expectations and Margot for protecting him. Margot faulted Jamie for not remaining "in denial" and blamed both her son and her husband for not being "man enough." Margot and Hank both sought to seal off Jamie's homosexuality. Eventually they ceased even to discuss it, and all elements of Jamie's life as a gay man were excluded from the life of the family.

This attempt to contain and encapsulate the child's same-sex orientation is a typical response of families in the disintegrated state. In our study, none of the families in this category had included in any significant way the lovers or friends of the gay child. In contrast, 64.3 percent of the ambivalent families and 100 percent of the integrated families included in their constellation their gay child's lovers or friends. Friends and lovers are typically shunned in families who are in the disintegration phase, their existence voided, because to acknowledge their place in the heart of the gay or lesbian child is to provoke the negative feelings that would violate the truce.

A gay man may be forced to pretend that his lover is a "friend," or his lover may be asked by his family to stay away on the holidays. The lesbian couple may be forced to choose between celebrating Thanksgiving separately or going to one partner's family's house and feeling lonely and unwanted. Unless there is a healthy reconciliation, the gay or lesbian adult child will in time withdraw from family get-togethers and holiday gatherings, in favor of their own "family of choice," where they feel more wanted and accepted.[2]

The flip side of externalizing shame by faulting others, as the Spauldings did, is to internalize it by faulting oneself. Many of the parents in the disintegrated phase revealed their internalized struggle with shame, as did Flora, talking about how her son, Kevin, first came out to her.

> In the beginning I wondered if there was anything I had done to make him [gay]. But you can have kids brought up in the same home, the same way, and one grows up to be a murderer. My son assured me that it was nothing I had done. [But] if he was retarded or a gay child it would all be something in my background or my husband's genetic

background that made him that way. So even though it wasn't the way I was with him, I still conceived—my poor little kid, it's still all my fault. I understand mothers who have deformed kids.

Flora's pain reveals so much about the effects of shame and stigma. She struggled with blaming herself and equating her son's sexual orientation with other heavily stigmatized identities: a murderer, or someone who is retarded or deformed. She saw herself or her husband as a genetic failure!

Bill, the father of a lesbian daughter, demonstrated other ways that shame could generate self-blame. A white, middle-class father of three, aged forty-three at the time of the interview, Bill had divorced his first wife and then remarried. A daughter from his first marriage, Jenny, twenty-three, had recently come out to him as a lesbian. He was shaken up by the news—obviously far more than he had anticipated. He felt ashamed of what his daughter had become and believed that his failed marriage had led to this outcome.

Bill was a successful businessman who had always devoted a lot of time to his work. Like many men of his generation, his work was his identity, and he sacrificed a great deal to achieve success, including his marriage. When Jenny was ten years old, he and his first wife separated and then, after an acrimonious period of blame, were divorced. The original family split apart. Bill withdrew from his children, feeling somewhat angry and guilty over the divorce. Later he regretted his withdrawal, but much of the damage had been done. The relationships with his children never recovered from this loss. The original family remained disintegrated.

In our interview Bill remembered Jenny's childhood fondly. She was "very athletic, very attractive, very intelligent, an all-American girl. She played sports and loved baseball. She was a good football player and an excellent runner. She qualified for all the best athletic teams." Bill was obviously proud of these things. However, he expressed guilt about his handling of Jenny. Years later, at the time of the interview, even though the divorce was seemingly completely separate from his daughter's coming out, Bill connected the events in his mind. Had he caused her lesbianism, he wondered? Guilty anxiety such as his was common to the narratives of parents in our study. Such feeling reflect the internalization of shame that comes from failing to live up to the Heterosexual Family Myth, as well as a desperate attempt to understand the reasons for the disruption of the Myth.

Bill recalled that he had wondered for a long time about Jenny's sexual orientation and had been suspicious. Was she "normal"? He had had strong negative feelings about homosexuals long before his daughter came out to him. They were filled with "stereotypes," Bill said, none of them positive.

At the time of the interview he experienced guilt about Jenny, complicated by shame. He believed that he had not been attentive enough to her, "not enough of a father." He described himself as having been "disconnected" from his daughter when she was growing up. Maybe he worked too much, he worried. He had liked Jenny to be in athletics but did not encourage her closeness to him. He wondered if he had favored his son over Jenny and she had felt "cheated by this." His suspicions that she might have felt "cheated" contributed to his sense that he had failed in his duties as a father.

His self-blame was persistent: perhaps he should have spent more time with her. Perhaps he made her a homosexual. Perhaps he should have discouraged her interest in sports—as if Jenny's athleticism somehow promoted her homosexuality. Perhaps he was "too hard on her." Yet he felt that even if he did "something to cause" her homosexuality, "it is too late to change it anyway; she is grown up."

But he never stopped loving her, Bill insisted. He reported that a long gap followed after the divorce when he and Jenny were out of touch. At the time of the interview their relationship was improving but, Bill said, "there is a long way to go" in gaining trust. He was working on changing his thinking about lesbians and gays, largely by going to PFLAG meetings and reading recommended literature. He was not so ashamed of Jenny's homosexuality as he had been at first, but he continued to search for causes in the past. He blamed his failed marriage as well as himself for his daughter's lesbianism. He fused the old guilt of a broken marriage with the newer sense of failure: perhaps if he had done things differently, he speculated, Jenny might have turned out heterosexual.

Richard and Betty Stein offer still another example of how shame can color a parent's response to a gay child's disclosure. The Steins were a Chicago suburban couple, married for many years. Richard was retired from the plumbing business, and Betty was a retired social worker. It was several years prior to our interview that they had first become aware of their youngest son acting "odd," as they described it. Rick had always been the most "sensitive" and "creative" of their three sons. But it was a shock when he came out to them. Betty recalled:

> I went through periods of guilt. I really felt like I was a total failure, that I had failed as a mother. I thought we fit the description of a domineering mother and weak or absent father. My husband was away from home much of the time and when he was home, he was so busy with the older boys, taking them to football games. They'd leave Rick with me, and since I enjoy the arts, I'd take him with me to art exhibits, sometimes even to fashion shows, to lunch with my lady friends. So I thought I had made a little girl out of my third son, because I never had a daughter and he was with me so much. So that whole Freudian concept gnawed at me, harassed me, punished me, and almost did me in, because I thought I had created a monster.

The emotional amphitheater is further complicated when negative feelings about a child's homosexuality exist within the context of guilt and blame toward oneself and one's spouse. Richard Stein admitted, "We were each blaming the other for causing Rick's condition. I was stunned, hysterical, bewildered. I wondered, 'Where did we go wrong? Who went wrong? What did we do?' We weren't sure whether it was a choice on his part or whether he was trying to hurt us." Clearly, one of the early common responses to the "monster" rearing its ugly head is to find the culprit. Every perceived failing of oneself, one's spouse, and one's child becomes suspect.

Another manifestation of shame is the fear some parents have of disclosing the sexual orientation of the child to others. The inability to share the information effectively deprives the family of sources of support, education, and encouragement. Among families that fell into the Disintegrated category in our study, only 11.1 percent had disclosed the information to at least one member of the extended family, and none had disclosed the information to two or more extended family members. Similarly, fewer families in the Disintegrated category than in the Ambivalent or Integrated categories had disclosed their child's homosexuality to a coworker or friend (although it appears that it was generally easier for families to disclose being the parent of a lesbian or gay child to friends and coworkers than to extended family).

Ralph, the policeman father we referred to earlier, described vividly his inhibitions about telling others. He did not seek help out of the family. When asked if he went to PFLAG, he responded, "I have never heard of it," and insisted, "I just don't want to be involved." He was very fearful that any of his fellow police officers might discover that he had a lesbian daughter. "It would be a shock if I were to go to a group and see someone else I knew. I'd die."

The mother of a gay son told us: "At the beginning I thought, 'What are people going to think?' It's my nature to not care whether people think one way or another. But it's strange: When it knocks on your own front door, suddenly you do see a stigma attached."

On occasion, parents were constrained from disclosing not because of their own fears or shame but because of those of the gay or lesbian child. One parent reported that although she would have liked to disclose her child's sexual orientation to other family members, her lesbian daughter's reluctance kept her from doing so. She made a pledge of secrecy to her daughter. Another father of a gay son told us that his son was afraid to come out to his older sister for fear that she would deprive him of a relationship to her children, his nieces and nephews.

Of course, the fear of disclosure is reinforced by the potential for negative consequences. Richard told us how he was interviewed by the local newspaper regarding his gay son and his support of gay human rights. The reporter, an older experienced man, was pleased with the interview. However, at the close he pondered for a moment and then said that he would not use Richard's real name in the story. When Richard was surprised, the Chicago reporter bluntly told him, "If I publish your real name, you might lose customers in your business." Long afterward, Richard recalled his shock and anger at realizing this. His situation was not unusual. To come out as the parent of a gay or lesbian is to deal with the same bigotry that meets the gay or lesbian person. It is that prejudice that produces shame in disintegrated families.

The shame or fear that parents may feel about a child's homosexuality leads them all too often to call upon inappropriate resources for help. Among the more heinous of these resources is the psychotherapist who holds out hope of "changing" a child's sexual orientation rather than showing the way to the process of integration. As one mother of a gay son confessed to us: "When I found out, I dumped on him. . . . I was terrible. I told him he was sick and that we needed to cure him. . . . I thought that he had chosen this and that his actions were sick. He said, 'whatever you want me to do, I'll do.' I subjected him to a lot—seeing psychiatrists—I dumped on him."

Attempts to change sexual orientation through certain kinds of therapy, sometimes called "reparative therapy," are potentially dangerous. The promises of "reparative therapy" are unproved. Most professional mental health organizations consider reparative therapy to be highly unethical. The American Psychiatric Association, which declassified homosexuality as a mental illness in 1974, stated as recently as 1993:

> There is no published scientific evidence supporting the efficacy of "reparative therapy" as a treatment to change one's sexual orientation. . . . There is no evidence that treatment can change a homosexual's deep-seated sexual feelings for others of the same sex. Clinical experience suggests that any person who seeks conversion therapy may be doing so because of social bias that has resulted in internalized homophobia, and that gay men and lesbians who have accepted their sexual orientation positively are better adjusted than those who have not done so.[3]

The American Academy of Pediatrics also stated in 1993: "Therapy directed specifically at changing sexual orientation is contraindicated, since it can provoke guilt and anxiety while having little or no potential for achieving changes in orientation."[4]

None of this is meant to discourage families from seeking counseling or psychotherapy as an additional tool to help them integrate their gay or lesbian child. Therapists who are truly knowledgeable can provide guidance and offer resources, and clarify any misconceptions the family may have. The skilled psychotherapist can also help the family to identify and utilize its own strengths to address the challenges inherent in integrating the lesbian or gay child into the family. The psychotherapist can provide a safe place for parents to express more fully all of their reactions. We have known several families who have successfully pursued just such a course.

The Notion of Sexual Orientation as a Phase

Unfortunately, families in a "Disintegrated" state may continue to deny the reality of having a gay child by insisting that his or her homosexuality is a "phase." The ploy is understandable because it is still widely held in our society, even by so-called experts, that homosexuality is just a phase in development to be passed through on the royal road to heterosexuality.[5] Such thinking derives from earlier notions that many adolescents pass through a stage of "sexual confusion" that may be characterized by sexual experimentation or unusually close relationships with the same sex. One mother said of her son's disclosure: "I thought it was a phase. Like being a Hare Krishna. 'So that's why we sent you away to college—so you could do these things!' I told him." The mother was not enlightened when she called a counselor to cope with the news. "I explained the situation to her. . . . She told me it was probably a phase."

Some of the parents we interviewed also described a period during which they believed that their child might be "bisexual." It is important to note here that true bisexuality, the experience of having quite equal attractions to both men and women, is a very real outcome of sexual orientation development for some. Others, however, may identify as bisexual on the way to developing a more consistent sexual orientation, gay or straight. Nonetheless, the fact that bisexuality has become more acceptable and prominent in our culture may pose a potential difficulty for parents struggling to accept their child's homosexuality. They may cling to a hope that their child will ultimately "cross over" to the heterosexual side. This may be a false hope and create more problems by delaying any efforts to integrate the homosexual child into the family.[6]

These strategies—blaming others or blaming oneself, avoiding disclosure, excluding the gay or lesbian child or their friends, denying reality, rationalizing the child's homosexuality as a phase—all have a disintegrating effect. They fragment relationships in the family, stultify personal growth, and make it increasingly difficult for the family to move toward integration.

We opened this chapter by quoting Betty Stein, who claimed she was close to "a nervous breakdown" when her son told her he was gay. We would like to close with Betty, by way of showing how much change is possible: Betty started with terrible fear and anger, but she gradually became accepting and found ways to integrate her son fully into the life of her family. Though it took several years, eventually—through support from the family and friends, by attending PFLAG and learning truths that are not included in the stereotypes about homosexuals, by meeting lesbians and gays for the first time—Betty and her husband, Richard, allowed themselves to take pride in their gay son, Rick. They were happy for what made him happy—his ability to live life as an openly gay man, his good relationship with his partner, his success in his career, his friends (gay, lesbian, and straight) by whom he is surrounded. Rick and his partner share their holidays and special time with each other's parents and siblings. The two men are valued members of both their families now. The Stein's story started in fragmentation but moved past disintegration and ambivalence to achieve what we can clearly call successful integration of their gay son into the family.

As the Steins discovered, disintegration need not be the end, but rather the beginning of a process of change, growth, and new development in parents. Betty and Richard have gone on to help other parents like themselves through their local PFLAG organization. They talk about how they came to deal with the "death" of their heterosexual son and his "rebirth" as a gay man. By their example, they teach other parents to do the same.

4

Somewhere in the Middle

Ambivalence

I wanted to see her with a family, the children, you know how parents feel. Then I began to realize that she is so capable—she'll be whatever she wants to be in life. Being gay doesn't faze her one way or the other—she's comfortable with it. That makes me feel good.

—*Ilene, fifty-eight-year-old mother of a lesbian daughter*

ILENE, WHEN WE INTERVIEWED HER, was at a point of a transition away from disintegration and the shame associated with not achieving heterosexual milestones. She was beginning to appreciate something deeper in her child, a quality that she respected and admired. From what she told us, it was clear to us that she was letting go of pre-conceived notions about what her daughter should be and was beginning to see and value who her daughter really was.

Ilene seemed to us to be in the phase we call "ambivalence." We placed parents in this category who were beginning to attempt to integrate their openly lesbian or gay children into their lives. These parents could, for example, see some positive aspects to learning that their child was gay. Their general attitude toward lesbians and gays was becoming more open. Several parents characterized their metamorphosis at this point:

> [Having a lesbian child] has made me understand that homosexuals are as human as heterosexuals and they have the same basic needs for survival as anyone else. And it has changed me in that I try to read and listen whenever I have the opportunity to find out what homosexuality is all about.

> I've became much more supportive to gay and lesbian activities, organizations, rights. It has helped me become a better parent.

However, the movement toward full integration of those parents we placed in the ambivalent category had met with only partial success. Some remained burdened by the stigma of having a gay or lesbian child:

> It's bothered me that I'm unable to relate this information to my brothers and sisters. I wonder what they think about gays in general and about [my son] in particular. The question comes up occasionally about him getting married. We just pass it off. I often feel if the question ever comes up about him being gay, I would say "yes," but I'm not going to volunteer this information.

It sure matured me fast. It changed my views. I'm much more tolerant. Still, I worry that I caused it. I have lots of guilt, even though . . .
I know all the right answers. I tell everyone they didn't do anything to
cause it. But deep down I feel like I'm this rotten mother.

Others expressed an awful fear for their child's future. When asked what
has been the greatest burden regarding their child's coming out, for
example, one father of a lesbian daughter remarked:

Thinking about all the crap she's going to have to deal with for the
rest of her life. She doesn't really deserve it because she's a neat person [tearful]. I feel so sad. She's very sensitive; obviously she's got
strength—coming out in high school—but I tend to think of her as
very vulnerable.

Still others described the struggle within the family to accept their gay
or lesbian child's same-sex partner. One mother recalled:

Joanne [my daughter] wanted to bring her partner, Maureen, for dinner. I had to tell the family that they could come, but no one else
wanted them to come. I was caught in the middle, but I stuck to my
decision. . . . Dinner was strained but we got through it okay.

More mothers than fathers in this group accepted their gay or lesbian offspring. One mother of a gay son reflected on her frustration
about her husband's progress toward greater acceptance: "My husband is having a difficult time with it. He's sad about his son, that he
isn't going to get married or have a child. I can fluff things off but my
husband is more serious. He keeps things inside. I wish he would be
more accepting."

Compared to most of the families discussed in the preceding
chapter, the parents in the category we call "ambivalent" were
betwixt and between—feeling less shame and more appreciation, but
only beginning to manifest this progress in their relationships with
others. Their voyage was still in process; they remained at sea in a
storm. They remained ambivalent about what to do and how far to
go in trying to make things better for themselves and their gay or lesbian children. In this way, they reflected the ambivalence of our present culture.

The Lowensteins: Portrait of an Ambivalent Family

Martin was a fifty-five year old father of four, a small businessman, who resided in a lower-middle-class suburban area of Chicago. He was a kind, gentle man, who suffered from several serious medical problems and was dismayed by the degree of conflict in his extended family. He had been married to his wife, Greta, for thirty years and had a daughter, Joan, and a son, Alec. Alec was twenty-four when he disclosed his homosexuality to to his parents. At the time of the interview, seven months had passed since the disclosure.

Martin and Greta had a good marriage, and it was a source of great support to Martin. Respect and care were evident in their interactions. They were Jewish, and Martin reported that religion and family were important values in his neighborhood. Simultaneously, negative attitudes about homosexuality, including open expressions of disgust, were also a part of their community. Alec lived at home and was working in Chicago at the time of his disclosure. The extended family had a history of conflict that preceded the difficulties it had in dealing with Alec's homosexuality. Martin's father, now quite elderly, did not approve of Martin's wife, Greta, and he had no relationship with Martin or Greta. Also, Martin and his sister no longer spoke because of family quarrels.

In growing up, Alec was not close to his father, according to Martin. He described their relationship as "not very strong" and said that they "took each other for granted." "Love is there," he commented, "but not expressed." They did not spend much time together. "I don't think I went out of my way to maintain a strong relationship." At best, they shared an interest in sports and went to baseball games together. "Looking back, there were times I could have extended myself more," But he noted that Alec was "always running, always going out. So we never got to see him much. He did his thing and we did our thing."

By contrast, he told us, Greta was close to Alec. Martin observed that Alec was "very special to her."

"She feels very good when he's around . . . they confide in each other a lot; he tells her much more than with me. I've turned him off as a listener. To me, it sounds like a bunch of nonsense, a bunch of jibber jabber." There was some resentment and hostility in this statement, but Martin also seemed aware of his feelings. "The problem" Martin said, is that "Alec was a loner," elusive; and while he lived at home, he hid "his problem," as Martin refers to Alec's homosexuality. The tendency in Martin that we could see at the time of the interview—to single out Alec's "problem"—reflected the ambivalence in the family.

Martin described a state of disintegration out of which his family had slowly begun to move. However, they seemed, at that point, not yet to operate as a strong and vital system. Alec, perhaps aware of his difference and fearful of rejection by his family, had learned early to avoid intimacy and be "elusive." The distance between father and son was palpable but not addressed. Greta seemed to provide the closeness and emotional support for Alec, and he confided in her. This fragile structure was sorely tested by Alec's coming out.

Within such a context, Alec chose a less direct means of communicating about his gay identity: he wrote a letter to his parents and gave it to them just before he left for the airport, on his way to San Francisco where he was going to join his lover.

According to Martin, the world caved in when he and his wife received the letter. Greta "completely fell apart." Nothing like this had ever happened to them before. "She was suicidal at the time," Martin recalled. "She couldn't stop crying." Greta was admitted to the local psychiatric hospital for ten days' observation and rest—on the orders of her family's personal physician. "She didn't really know how bad she felt. She was really destroyed," Martin reiterated.

After they got to the emergency room, Martin called the airline and had Alec paged in order to tell him to come to the hospital immediately. Instead of worrying about the shape she was in, Martin said, "My wife wanted the doctors to change Alec, to change his homosexuality." This was, in fact, the first thing Greta demanded of her own doctor. When the doctor said he could not "fix" Alec, Greta was overcome with grief. Martin recalled that she went into a "complete panic, brow-beating herself because of her guilt." Martin, by contrast, had to remain cool in order to help his wife and get through the crisis. But by doing so, he bottled up his own feelings, which were painfully slow to come out.

Alec did come to the hospital from the airport. His father described the drama that ensued as "a tough scene":

> My wife was trying to get Alec fixed back [to being heterosexual]. So Alec left us at the hospital, and she was then placed on antidepressants and remained in the psychiatric ward, because they were afraid that

she might harm herself. After she was released, we went to a private psychiatrist for four sessions. It really was a waste, because he could offer nothing but consolation. He said also they couldn't "fix" Alec. The dirty deed was done . . . and then Alec just left us feeling very sad. A very deep wound was inflicted.

From his intonation it was clear that Martin was still angry about his son's revelation. He seemed to be blaming Alec still for the family turmoil—not a very auspicious development if the family was to be healed.

Alec, feeling burdened with guilt and distraught over the dramatic turn of events, felt compelled to move out of his parents' home precipitously, for the first time in his life. "After that hospital scene, we didn't hear from him again," Martin recalled. The degree of avoidance, anxiety, and guilt was great on both sides. To pick up his mail, Alec would come to the house when everyone else was gone in order to escape direct confrontation. All communication ceased, and it appeared that the fragile structure of the family had nearly collapsed. Perhaps the saving grace was that Alec and his sister, Joan, stayed in contact and she was supportive of him.

Martin's account of the next period, though, indicated a perceptible (if slight) change in his attitude:

> It was a bad scene when he did this. . . . There was just a natural buildup of anxiety, and guilt. He was full of guilt. He knew he had hurt us badly. Me and my wife talked after the initial shock . . . we discussed the hurt that Alec must have felt. And society, they don't take it kindly.

Martin's ambivalence was wavering toward consolation and support. Yet he and his son avoided each other for three months. Then, Martin and Greta called Alec. Perhaps, given the history of their previous conflicts with extended family, Martin and Greta were particularly motivated to do all they could to keep their own nuclear family together; they did not wish to suffer the same alienation from their son as they had from other family members. Martin described the first attempt at reconciliation:

> My wife spoke to him, and then I did. We set up a dinner appointment. I was very fearful about this meeting. He later called us that

very morning, reconfirming the appointment. The meeting was very positive. I set the tone for the meeting. I told him about the feeling of me and my wife. . . . I expressed our feeling for him, and that we wouldn't reject him. Things got better, tolerable. There were telephone calls on a weekly basis.

Yet, though Martin was willing to make some move toward integration, he could not fully reconcile himself to his son's homosexuality. He claimed that he feared that bad things would happen to Alec because he was gay—AIDS was uppermost in his mind, though he tried not to express his anxiety too often: "I'm still fearful of saying something that will ruffle his feathers . . . that can ruin our relationship again," Martin told us. He also feared homophobia: "When society eventually finds out," Martin lamented, "it could hurt him."

At that point, Martin and Greta had not come out to their friends or family. The extent of their isolation was painful to him. "I am troubled by my loneliness about it. It's something you have to deal with yourself, to make yourself happy." Martin was so fearful of the opinions and reactions of others that he felt compelled to bear the burden alone. Such silence is characteristic among families in both the disintegration and ambivalence phases. Communication is cautious, and "dead zones" emerge where topics or feelings are taboo.

Martin continued to feel some shame over his son's homosexuality. At times he was so overcome by strong emotions in the interview that he would mumble and be incoherent. We would have to ask him to repeat what he said. He was unable to utter the word "gay" during an entire two-hour interview. He also expressed muted anger by saying, paradoxically, that his son "betrayed the family all those years" by not telling them of his homosexuality. This laying of blame on a gay child, characteristic of families in the disintegrated phase who are also struggling with shame, was tempered by Martin's nascent awareness that it is society, the cultural milieu, that may be culpable. He remarked that he was not sure "how to handle people in society when they find out about my son" and acknowledged how difficult it must be for Alec because "society looks down on [his homosexuality] as so bad."

When asked how Alec's disclosure had affected Martin's relationship with Greta, Martin said that they want the best for their son but have a hard time dealing with his homosexuality. "We're not enthralled by it. We're not in favor of it. We'd do anything to alter it. We'd love to have more grandchildren." Their daughter Joan's children, he said "take away some of the pain of Alec's condition."

But Martin also observed: "I can see nothing but positiveness coming out of this whole thing. We're novices to this . . . as we mature, within this thing, it will make it easier on Alec with parents who love him."

Martin's capacity to project himself to a time of greater peace was a hopeful sign. His determination, however, was still more intellectual than emotional. "We're not the happiest people in the world. Who the hell can be happy about it?" he said with a tinge of anger. But then he added, almost in reaction to his own thoughts: "Alec seems more at peace now. The load has been taken off his back. We're delighted that he seems to be at peace and that we have a relationship with our son. It could have gotten much worse, and it could have made us lose our son, due to our ignorance."

Clearly, although the Lowensteins came to the brink of a rupture, they found their way back. In spite of Greta's extreme reaction and hospitalization, the parents' pain and shame, their repudiation of their son and his subsequent withdrawal from the family household, these people managed to come back together. Greta recovered, and the couple reached out to their son, beginning with their invitation to dinner. Martin reasserted his paternal role by expressing his love and affection for Alec. Martin and Greta sought support outside of the family by becoming members of PFLAG, the support group for parents and friends of lesbians and gays. Most important, they expressed in the interview their hope that their progress would continue.

Some Differences Between the Responses of Fathers and Mothers in Ambivalent Families

Progress toward integration may be impeded by the fact that, in many American families, fathers exercise power through setting boundaries and rules governing interactions both within the family and between the family and the external world. In this sense, perhaps, fathers internalize the ideal norms of the culture and feel obliged to uphold the rules within their own families. By setting more restrictive boundaries in dealing with a gay or lesbian child, fathers may be more likely than mothers to inhibit integration. We observed particularly adamant restrictions in fathers who were upset about their daughter's lesbianism. As one father remarked of his lesbian daughter, "If she's gay, she's gay. I don't approve of this stuff. We kind of have this understanding. Don't throw this stuff in my face. I don't want her to bring her gay friends over."

A significant difference between the response of the father to a child's lesbianism and that of the mother was illustrated for us in our interview with Gladys and James, an African-American couple whose daughter, Cathy, had fallen in love with Dionne, her first significant romantic relationship. While James was hostile to Cathy's partner, Gladys complained not about Cathy and Dionne but about James:

> Discussions are usually triggered if Dionne comes to visit. His comments aren't very nice. I can't understand why he blames Dionne, and that causes disagreement. It just doesn't go away. The person Cathy loves is scapegoated. That's unfair. So we get into it. Yes, in the beginning there were rough times, negative energies. He seemed to have shameful, guilty, negative feelings about it, and no coping abilities. He thought I should've been feeling the same way. Even now, the problem is still about Dionne!

We also found that fathers in the ambivalent phase were more likely than mothers to draw a line by preventing disclosure to people outside the immediate family, including grandparents, aunts, or uncles. Generally, we discovered that fathers were reluctant to seek any help or support outside the family. The fact that it was typically harder to coax fathers into disclosing their story to us in this study may well derive from the same motivation.

We were especially curious about why fathers seemed to have so much more difficulty with lesbian daughters than the mothers did. In our study, mother/daughter relationships were almost twice as "integrated" as father/daughter relationships. While it is risky to draw conclusions from so small a sample, themes emerge from our interviews that provide clues.

On a psychological level, we wonder if a father may regard a daughter's attraction to other women as a rejection of himself as a man. In this sense the father feels he has failed to establish the "desirability" of men as objects or sources of mature love and affection. A father may determine he has failed in his role if his daughter does not aspire to marry a man "like my father." But as Ann Muller reported with regard to parents' response to a child's homosexuality in general, mothers typically experienced hurt and loss, while fathers became angry, broke off communication, and sometimes severed all bonds.[1] It is likely that this extreme reaction is driven ultimately by the profound role pressures exerted upon fathers by society.

Fathers' reactions to gay sons may play out differently from their reactions to lesbian daughters. Fathers of gay sons seem more likely to ascribe the label of "failure" to both themselves and their sons. If a boy did not aspire to share activities with his father or aspired to share in his mother's culture, the child's gayness may be interpreted in retrospect as being the result of a failure by the father who feels that he was an inadequate role model. The father may also charge his son with having failed to aspire to his proper gender role. Many gay sons, consequently, struggle initially to overcome a profound sense of inadequacy or failure as men. Such themes, which revolve around anxieties concerning proper gender behavior, are strongly reinforced by the culture and are often reiterated in family stories about who is "to blame."

Mothers, in contrast, tend to focus more on relational features, such as how they must now interact with their children. They struggle more to keep the family together. They feel the need to overcome differences in the family and to maintain the bonds of love and devotion regardless of disappointments. In this sense the mother may bury her own feelings, take on the task of being the Great Mediator, or try to deflect blame from others on to herself. Mothers, we have found, are less likely to reject out of hand their gay and lesbian offspring, even if that child fails to fulfill their most heartfelt hopes and dreams, as illustrated earlier by Greta Lowenstein.

As we discovered in our interviews, while a number of mothers spoke of being disappointed in their lesbian daughters or gay sons, their full rejection was rare. Indeed, we had no example of it among the mothers we studied. However, the issues of grandchildren and of general disappointment in the gay or lesbian child continued to compromise the reactions of mothers in the ambivalent phase. They had not yet fully reconsidered the Heterosexual Family Myth, and they suffered because their gay or lesbian children were not adhering to the cultural ideal that the Myth demanded.

A Word About Gender Roles and "The Cause"

It is not unusual for some fathers to enjoy periods of great closeness in their early relationships with daughters. The closeness is sometimes pursued through typically "male" interests, such as sports. If the daughter comes out as a lesbian, a father sometimes worries that there is a connection between her sexuality and their early closeness and activities. Ralph could not hide that fear when he spoke to us of his lesbian daughter, Janie:

> I wanted a daughter very bad. She was my little girl. She still is. For the first six months of her life, I don't think my wife ever had to change the diapers. I did it all. Later we took walks, went shooting, fishing, played sports. My wife thinks that Janie's being a lesbian may be because me and Janie participated in everything that was male. If that close contact has anything to do with her sexual orientation in relating to male figures . . . maybe I should have been more distant.

While we found a variety of instances in which lesbian daughters like Janie or gay sons like Rick Stein exhibited nonconforming gender behavior, we believe that the relationships the parents formed with them were more in *response* to these differences, which were at least partly inherent and which the parents perceived when the child was young.

Both mothers and fathers in our interviews appeared confused about the "cause" of homosexuality. Several of them feared that it was related to the child's learning inappropriate gender behaviors when young. Mothers sometimes expressed dismay when they recalled their daughter's aspirations to share in "men's activities"—which the mothers saw as "a problem" once the girl entered adolescence. Several fathers falsely concluded, as did Ralph, that the moments of great fun and intimacy that they shared with their young daughter somehow caused her to become lesbian. With regard to their gay sons, mothers similarly expressed guilt or remorse for having shared with them gender non-conforming interests (shopping, arts, music, fashion), as we saw from Betty Stein's testimony in chapter 3. They too concluded wrongly that these experiences somehow "caused" their sons to "turn out gay."

From our observations and research, we believe it is safe to say unequivocally that parents' behavior (e.g., Ralph taking Janie fishing) in no way promotes or causes the development of same-sex sexual orientation. A child's gender and sexual development are not just "planted" in the child by the parent or the culture. Sexual and gender development do not begin with a blank slate. Development is multidetermined and multidirectional. It involves what comes from the child and how the child responds to the cues in the world (including what the parents do, but also what peers do and the *meanings* ascribed to various patterns and behaviors by the culture).[2]

While we cannot know the complex unconscious patterns that occur in families, nevertheless, lesbian daughters and gay sons—like all children—express their own feelings, interests, likes, dislikes, and subjective desires all the time in growing up. These do not completely, or perhaps even primarily, depend upon what their parents do or do not do. Indeed, it is likely that parents react to intrinsic qualities within their children.[3] In effect, some fathers may reject sons (consciously or unconsciously) who do not indicate strong interest in traditional male-identified activities, such as sports. Mothers may quite naturally feel more drawn to these sons because of common interests. Similarly, mothers may have difficulty relating to daughters who do not conform to more old-fashioned female gender role behavior, whereas fathers may initially delight in such relationships with their daughters. Clearly, the culture is changing in this area. But there is no hard evidence whatsoever that such parent/child relationships *cause* homosexuality. Nor should this discussion suggest that all gay men or lesbians were gender nonconforming in childhood. In fact, many were gender typical. But the point we wish to reiterate and emphasize is that there is nothing to suggest that father/daughter or mother/son bonding ever causes a particular sexual orientation—gay, straight, or bisexual.

Disclosure

Ambivalent families demonstrate tremendous conflict regarding disclosure to others about their child's homosexuality. Because accessing support from others is so critical, the inability to disclose that a child is lesbian or gay can seriously inhibit the family's advance toward integration. Shame, fear and embarrassment unfortunately prevent families from taking this necessary step, as seen from the example of the Lowensteins.

A particularly poignant aspect of avoidance is the parents' concern about disclosing to their own parents and to other members of their extended family. Like all other elements of society, the larger family, including the grandparents, can be positive or negative about the gay or lesbian child. Parents often feel trepidation, however, that their own parents (the child's grandparents) will judge them and find them unworthy as parents. The extended family may be a source of grief and anger for parents, since relatives outside the nuclear family have less knowledge of the gay child, less of a stake in understanding the situation, and less commitment to integrating the child back into the family.

But sometimes a parent's reluctance to disclose can be based more in fear than in reality. For example, we noted that grandparents were able in some cases to be more accepting than their own children! Grandparents can be agents of integration—if they are allowed to know the truth. After all, they have little to gain by rejecting their grandchildren, and they stand to lose the very thing—grandchildren—that provides such meaning to their lives.

Cynthia, who is forty, and her husband Bill, forty-two, were interviewed separately in our study, at about the same time that we interviewed their nineteen-year-old son, David. They are professional people who live in Chicago. They had always had a very positive relationship to their son. The couple did not suspect that David was gay prior to his coming out. Cynthia's family was not very religious, but her husband's family was religiously conservative.

David had come out to his parents the year before the interview and, in general, their response was positive but guarded. He was their only son and was much loved and admired by his parents. The family always had experienced warm, intimate relations, without interruption. When David went off to college he soon formed a significant romantic relationship with another man at his school. But Cynthia could not accept this development so quickly: "When David wanted to pierce his ears, for example, I thought it was okay at first, but then I became afraid people would see and think something was wrong with him." His maternal grandparents were long unaware of any of these events. But eventually they discovered that David was living with a man, and they began to draw their own conclusions. Cynthia recalled:

> Initially I thought my parents would think it is a terrible thing to have a gay son, like at one time it was a mental illness; you had to keep it secret, it was shameful. Shocking. I didn't want them to suffer! Yes, when it involved my own parents, it seemed more shameful.

In fact, however, they took the news in their stride and were quite accepting of David, who was very appreciative of their support.

But not everyone in Cynthia's family was positive, she noted: "I even found out about a year ago, that my sister, whom I previously thought was on my son's side, let it be known that she thought two men or two women together sexually was disgusting." Cynthia drifted away from a close relationship with her sister. That was the "fall out" of David's coming out. But neither Cynthia or her husband seemed perturbed by it. Cynthia revealed far more ambivalence about her in-laws, the other side of the family. At one point in our interview with her, she said:

We still haven't told Bill's parents [David's other set of grandparents]. They will probably never know. I'm leaving it up to Bill. He doesn't want them to know and neither does David, primarily for religious reasons. You see, Bill's parents are Southern Baptists. I've never heard them say homosexuality is a bad thing, but it's believed by many in the Southern Baptist church and David went to Church camp there. The first speech he heard at camp was a tirade against homosexuality, saying they are sinners and go to hell. I don't care whether they know or not. My fear is that instead of rejecting David, they would be hassling us to take him to a psychiatrist or to pray for him—get him into religious groups that purport to convert people to heterosexuality. Bill thinks [his parents] would be very hurt by it and he doesn't want them to experience that. He's not ready yet to deal with their questions and anxiety.

Cynthia and Bill were thus in a situation parallel to that of gay children—fearful of failing to fulfill their own parents expectations! But then the secret got out anyway—the cycle was interrupted—as typically happens. Cynthia subsequently told us, "Dealing with my husband's part of the family has been hard. They were brutal. My husband's brother wrote a letter to my gay son saying our son was a 'disgrace' to the family. My mother-in-law turned against [my son] then. My husbands' sister told our son that by telling his grandmother about his sexual orientation, he has hastened her death." Such cruel responses are sometimes inevitable.

Even close friends can become the source of ambivalence. As Gladys related, "I have a friend who I think wants to ask me about my [lesbian] daughter. Our children were raised together. I think the word's gotten back to her but she doesn't say anything. One time I think she remarked, 'I don't know why you let Cathy go to the University—people are crazy over there!' I think she was trying to say something indirectly."

Gladys implied that her friend believed that simply being in the University might cause her daughter to become a lesbian. "I responded, 'Cathy went to school where she wanted to go.' I almost retaliated with words about my friend's bad marriage and her problems with her own children, but I held my tongue. Right then I was feeling angry." Gladys's angry response to her friend suggests that her ambivalence is changing into unqualified support.

Grief and Loss

It is in the phase of ambivalence that parents of gay and lesbian offspring can begin to grieve over what they cannot help but feel is their loss. Families in the disintegrated phase, entrenched in an array of defenses, are unable to do so because they refuse to acknowledge the reality. Families in the ambivalent phase, because they make that acknowledgement and continue to communicate with each other and those beyond the family, take the first steps. The experience of loss is indeed profound for most families, since most are invested in supporting and living out the cultural ideals of being heterosexual. These families must acknowledge that life will be different. And even now, when gay men and lesbians are having children through adoption, surrogacy, or donor insemination, or when same-sex couples are having commitment ceremonies, and gay marriage may even be legalized, for many parents homosexual relationships will still be stigmatized.[4] Parents need time to acclimate to this new reality and grieve for the loss of the realization of those heterosexual ideals in which they have so greatly invested. The ambivalence phase affords them that time and, with appropriate support, families can progress.

Equally important, we have found that this progress is greatly affected by the progress of the gay or lesbian child. Many parents told us how they could not help but be reassured by seeing their child in a positive emotional state at the point of disclosure, despite the parents' own fears and misgivings. In our study, almost 70 percent of the ambivalent families could acknowledge their child's improved state and sense of happiness, compared to only 22 percent of the disintegrated families The comfort that a child displays with regard to his/her own sexual orientation can inspire confidence, for the child will in many ways lead the parents out of the thicket of dread and confusion.

It also appears critical that offspring who are "out" to their families remain "out." By continuing to integrate their same-sex orientation into their lives, by developing friendships with other lesbians and gay men, by pursuing positive activities in the gay or lesbian community, by continuing to address the effects of homophobia on their lives and on their relationships, and by including these elements in their relationships with family members, gay and lesbian offspring ensure that their families are less likely to return to a disintegrated state of silence, secrecy and shame. Rather, families are then challenged to continue the work and foster greater dialogue. Moreover, although some parents may initially balk at having their child's sexual orientation "thrown in our faces," the more resilient among them regard the challenge as an opportunity for further growth and differentiation. Indeed, they come to see that their gay or lesbian offspring aren't "flaunting" anything per se, but simply laying claim to the same right as heterosexuals to incorporate key elements of their lives.

Families overcome their ambivalence through this willingness on the part of both the child and the parents to be honest with each other, to respect differences, to be uncomfortable even for long periods of time, and, ultimately, to construct new meanings of sexuality, love, adversity, and family.

5

The Family Renewed

Integration

I think that he is more himself now. It's like, will the real Jonathan stand up? And he has! And there is something wonderful about that!
—Joan, mother of a gay son

The best thing about having a gay child is, if you have accepted your gay child, you find an outpouring of love from the child and his friends and the gay community. You get back a hundredfold what you give your child.
—Belinda, mother of a gay son

IN THE PREVIOUS CHAPTERS we described the disintegrating impact of the shame that some parents of gay and lesbian children told us they felt. As we discussed, it is clear that old cultural ideals have not yet caught up with the realities of contemporary society. We also looked at families betwixt and between, struggling to stay intact and overcome the damage wrought by secrecy and alienation. Despite the sadness and disappointment inherent in some of their stories, we found much to learn from them, often in the way of "cautionary tales."

While the stories of disintegration illustrate the difficulties that parents of gay and lesbian children face, those of integration, which we will discuss in this chapter, provide a beacon of hope. As the parents we placed in the integrated category understood, despite the cultural ideal of heterosexuality, you do not have a choice regarding the sexual orientation of your child; you do, however, have a momentous choice about how to respond to his or her orientation.

Before parents can replace negative responses with understanding and acceptance of their child's homosexuality, they must cope with their feeling of loss when they discover that one of the family members is gay or lesbian. It is not unusual that their immediate reaction is one of unhappiness. They fear what the extended family and friends will say; they fear that society will impose reprisals against their child; they may anticipate trouble with their church; they are very unhappy and even angry over the feeling that they may never have the grandchildren they had hoped for. These reactions are inevitable as long as one continues to be imprisoned by the cultural image of the heterosexual family, a particular mythology more suited to the 1950s than to today's era of diversity and individuality. The pressures imposed by this Myth forces parents to feel they must continue to hide "family secrets" from the outside world. They are constrained to pretend that everything is "normal." The price they pay is fragmentation, alienation, and the loss of meaningful family ties.

But the challenge they must undertake, for the sake of their children and for their own sake, is to create a supportive and more loving family, based upon reality and the acceptance of people as they are. In our interview with her, Louise demonstrated how parents can, and do, undertake that challenge. When she discovered her son David's homosexuality, the jolt was great, but ultimately she found ways to react that differed dramatically from those of the ambivalent parents of our last chapter. Louise did not hide from us the shock she felt when she first learned about David's sexuality:

> I found out at Thanksgiving. He called and told us he was gay. He had strong feelings then and they had lasted the longest. It was like he was a different person; he wasn't the son I had known and raised. It was almost as if a gypsy came and took away my real son and brought this one. He seemed so strange to me. I felt guilty.

She also did not hide from us the difficult struggle that she went through to find ways to accept David's disclosure:

> I was pretty well educated about homosexuality. I figured if no one knows what causes it, why should I blame myself? Maybe I did do something, but then that means I would have had to have raised him differently. But how could I do that being who I am? So those thoughts lasted maybe a day. But the feeling that he was a stranger lasted for months. I even thought about maybe having had another [person's] baby [laugh], a cuckoo bird lays its egg in another bird's nest. So he hatched out into something totally unexpected.

Yet it was her ability to listen to David that ultimately permitted her to see the situation as he saw it—in a way that was often more rational than her perceptions had permitted her to be. Through listening to him with love and openness, she was able to overcome her anachronistic cultural ideal in coming to terms with his understanding of himself:

> He was the one who helped me get over [my first bad feelings]. At Christmas, whenever I needed him to be there, he was. I told him how I felt. He was very kind. I said something to him about some moms having sorrow about not having grandchildren, and David said, "Mom, I'm only eighteen. I'm too young to be a parent!" The guilt went away pretty quick. I didn't really feel there was anything to feel guilty about. If scientists said you did one thing and that caused it, then maybe I'd feel guilty. My thinking has changed. More and more

I've come to accept that it's okay, so there is nothing to feel guilty about. That's how I feel now. If I could wave a magic wand and make him straight, I don't know if I would. Then he really would be different, and I like him the way he is.

Louise concluded with a rationality that mirrored the truth and also permitted her growth and happy reconciliation with her son:

I had to accept it—there's nothing I can do about it. I even came to look on it as a positive thing. There's nothing wrong with it. When he first came out, in a balance between straight and gay, I would have preferred straight. But through getting more involved in gay issues and knowing more gay people, that's changed.

How Parents Can Make a Difference

Louise was not unique in her acceptance of her gay son. Integrated families are those who have been able to find ways to transcend the "issue" of having a lesbian or gay child so that they can get on with life. The families may continue to have difficulties and conflicts, of course, because that's the nature of family life. Yet problems are no more likely to be related to having gay or lesbian offspring than to any other dimension of family life. Integrated families have enhanced communication both within the family and beyond. They can be open with others about having a gay or lesbian child. They take risks in disclosing their experiences to others. Integration of the gay child promotes this growth.

Marital and sibling relationships also appeared stronger in those families we placed in the "integrated" category. It seemed to us that often the family was strong not so much in spite of the conflicts posed by the homosexual child's disclosure but because of them. Even in those marriages that displayed the greatest strength prior to disclosure, parents often spoke of a new-found respect for each other—as if they had rediscovered their reasons for liking one another. Integrated families also reported significant improvement in the relationships between the gay child and the parents. The family wounds brought about by prior fragmentation and disintegration healed.

In particular, the integration process restarted the normal process of maturation and growth that is so crucial to the child's development into a fully functioning adult. Experts in the field of developmental psychology now recognize the significance of a child's ability, primarily during adolescence and young adulthood, to separate successfully from his or her parents and to individuate—that is, to become an autonomous, self-directed person with a substantially defined identity that has matured beyond the child's earlier role in the family. This complex set of tasks is marked initially by the child's identification with his or her family and parents. He or she subsequently shifts these allegiances to the norms and beliefs of his or her peers, constructing a personal passage toward a more distinct self-identity. Particularly at the entry into adolescence, acceptance by peers carries a profound sense of belonging and identification with a new society. This process of friendship and peership generates a new sense of self—of being separate from the familial identity of son or daughter, brother or sister. As the child matures, he or she claims new-found confidence, pride, and growth from the emerging sense of self in society.

The peer-group identity is reinforced by teen preferences for certain tastes, styles of clothing or jewelry, particular fads in music or art, the choice of particular words and idiomatic expressions. As silly and superficial as these things may seem, they generate a strong sense of belonging that paradoxically ensures psychological safety for adolescents as they separate from the attachment to parents. Each new peer-group identity constitutes a bridge of confidence toward an autonomous and more richly defined self. This new sense of self may cause young people to begin to reclaim from the family what was previously set aside. Ultimately, as adolescents become young adults, they can synthesize from both the peer-group identity and their familial identity a unique set of values, beliefs, and interests. They make choices more freely and develop a capacity for intimacy and commitment in both friendship and romantic relationships.

In the normative process of adolescence in Western culture, the parent-child relationship is transformed as well. It expands in order to recognize and incorporate the emergent young adult. It becomes increasingly a relationship between equals. Parent and child distribute power more evenly and accept and respect their differences more readily. The parent relinquishes authority as the adult child now exercises a greater range of choices and, ideally, accepts greater responsibility. Ultimately, parents "let go" and accept the reality of having "launched" their child into the world. Hoping they have given the child both the wisdom and the psychological resources necessary for a good life, parents acknowledge the limits of their control over the destiny of their child. In response, the adult child charts his or her own path of career, lifestyle, and attachments. Ultimately, the family incorporates the adult child's new identity into itself, including the child's romantic partner and family.

For lesbians and gay men, this normal process is too often thwarted due to the rejection, isolation, and stigma they so often experience during childhood and adolescence. Due to the taboos of society, lesbian and gay teens are unlikely to disclose their sexual orientation to peers or family, at least not until late adolescence. Many learn to create for themselves a variety of masks, images, or "false selves" in order to communicate with others. Their inner desires remain concealed, however, to avoid suspicion. The peer group, that bridge of psychological security described earlier, may be extremely hostile to homosexuality and is treacherous at best for the gay or lesbian teen. Whatever acceptance comes from peers has strings attached and is often at great cost to the self. Usually, acceptance can be gained only through deceit, denial, concealment, and the construction of this mask and false self. In short, struggling gay or lesbian teens must reject their own self in order to avoid rejection by others. The need to conceal the self becomes even more critical in the face of violence and harassment—so common in high school—especially for those labeled "dyke" or "fag."

Immobilized by fear, few gay and lesbian adolescents can engage in the more normative functions of adolescent socialization, except perhaps for those fortunate enough to access gay and lesbian youth programs in larger cities. But even in major metropolises, that is rare: only one out of forty-five homosexual teens in Chicago are that fortunate. What lesbian and gay teens are generally deprived of, therefore, are those normative functions that help adolescents to become socialized: discussing their feelings with friends for long hours on the phone; trading confidences with steady dates; learning the subtleties of dating, and so on. Most gay and lesbian youth—deprived by society, forced to hide who they are, feeling and being isolated—thus fail to develop the crucial skills of partner selection, communication, intimacy, and commitment by the end of their teenage years.

Equally important, many lesbian and gay young adults may have immense difficulty accomplishing the necessary psychological separation from their parents. Lacking the peer group bridge, some may remain excessively dependent on their parents for emotional support and comfort. Others may feel guilty and may experience a burdensome need to compensate their parents for failing to fulfill the heterosexual role expectations of marriage and children. These gay men and lesbians become and remain "best little boys" and "best little girls." Parents may rely on them unduly. This reliance denies that the parent must recede in a child's life. All this prolonged (sometimes mutual) dependence typically occurs in the context of hiding the self, of keeping the family secret.

Robb Forman Dew, the author of the autobiographical work, *The Family Heart: A Memoir of When Our Son Came Out*, has described—in terms all too familiar to us because it echoed what we often heard in our interviews—her own family's experiences with a gay son's assumption of the "best little boy" role. To assume that role he had to repress and deny himself, at considerable cost:

> Stephen has always had astonishing social radar, and I can see now with horrified clarity that he absorbed the idea of responsibility for the happiness of his own parents like a sponge. I think that it must have been at a huge cost to himself that he made it so easy for us to be pleased to be his parents. . . . He became what he thought he needed to be in order to ensure our satisfaction with ourselves as parents. He is, though, who he is; he never compromised his integrity or his character; instead he denied himself freedom of affection, the euphoria of early crushes, the experimentation of early emotional attachments. *(150)*

Some gay or lesbian teens, in a misguided effort to overcome their unresolved dependency on parents, may leave home prematurely. The gay or lesbian adolescent who runs away in order to achieve a sense of independence before garnering the necessary skills and resources to do so is rendered vulnerable to exploitation, crime, and sexually transmitted disease. Research into youth homelessness in one metropolitan city, Chicago, indicates that as many as 40 percent of homeless youth are gay-identified or homosexually active (often engaging in prostitution for economic survival).

How do parents in integrated families manage to overcome the various potential dangers and pitfalls to which families of young lesbians and gays are subject? Many of those who have been the most successful not only accept their child's same-sex orientation but also articulate an appreciation of it. We have no reason to think that this positive reaction derives from some special affection for homosexuality. Rather, we think that it is the result of the parents' willingness to go the extra step. They want to attend to the things that the child loves and appreciates in his or her own life. Thus, for example, they may include the partner of their gay or lesbian offspring into their family, or they may develop relationships with the partner's family. They may make efforts to learn more about lesbians and gay people in history, or about gay and lesbian communities.

What can we expect of such attempts at integration? Results that are surely happier than what we can observe in disintegrated or ambivalent families. As a consequence of taking active steps to learn more about the lives of lesbian and gay people, for example, it became easier for parents in integrated families to project a hopeful future for their gay or lesbian children. Among our interviewees, almost 77 percent of parents in the integrated category could project major life events for their gay children for at least ten years into the future. This contrasts with 41 percent of the "ambivalent" parents and none of the parents in the "disintegrated" category. Integrated parents could, therefore, more readily engage with their children in shared problem-solving and planning for life.

The narratives of these parents were striking. Many expressed a sort of gratitude for the gift of compassion that having a gay child afforded them. One mother of a gay son said with pride:

> This broadened my world. It's made me a better person. We do help other people that are coming out—you're much more sensitive to other people's concerns. I feel lucky compared to some other parents.

The father of a gay son told us:

> It has made me more human because I've become aware of a segment of society that's been treated very badly by government and the majority of the population. It's made me more compassionate toward those who've been persecuted. It's been very humanizing.

Another mother of a gay son completed the phrase: "The best thing about having a gay child is . . ." by saying:

You have accepted your gay child, [and] you find an outpouring of love from the child, his friends and the gay community. You get back a hundredfold what you give your child.

"Disintegrated" or "ambivalent" families more typically limited their exposure to, or involvement with, key aspects of the lives of their gay children. The parents were generally reluctant to include the child's gay or lesbian friends in family activities, or they did not want to encounter their adult child's partner. In contrast, parents in integrated families spoke positively of including into their lives those who were important in their child's life. Such inclusion rewarded the parents by fostering their feelings of closeness to their homosexual children.

As one mother of a gay son, Daniel, voiced it: "When I look ahead I see a good life for me and I look forward to closeness with Daniel and a continued relationship with Joey [his lover] or new people Daniel might bring into his life." The mother of a lesbian told us: "I like the community she lives in. I like her friends and enjoy them thoroughly. I enjoy being with them and doing things together." A father, discussing the relationship between his gay son and his wife, laughingly remarked: "It always was excellent. The only thing that's changed is that now she's trying to get him boyfriends instead of girlfriends. My wife has introduced him to nice people she had become friends with in the gay community." It is undeniable that these parents in integrated families were far happier than the father of the lesbian daughter that we discussed earlier who complained, "I don't approve of this stuff. . . . Don't throw this stuff in my face. I don't want her to bring her gay friends over."

The parents in integrated families that we interviewed believed it was important to weave a lesbian or gay child into the fabric of extended family relationships. They were less willing to hide or conceal from people who were important to them the fact of their child's homosexuality. Daniel's mother remarked with relief: "I'm glad we told my parents; Daniel is not drifting from them anymore; he can talk to them." Parents in integrated families believed it was vital to claim their child, not to let the possible prejudices of the extended family, neighborhood, church or even close friends wedge their child apart from them.

Of course, such openness on the part of these parents sometimes created conflicts with others outside their nuclear family. Yet integrated parents took the risks and held firm to their position. Though in some cases their defense of their child even caused them to be alienated from members of their extended family, it was not unusual for them to find that their courage paid off. Betty Stein, who moved from the ambivalent state described in chapter 4 to integration, recalled for us a potentially painful situation she and Richard, her husband, faced when they insisted on the inclusion of the lover of her gay son, Rick, at a family event:

> My brother was planning a wedding for his daughter and my husband announced to my brother that he wanted a young man placed on the invitation list. My brother said he was not inviting any friends of guests, only husbands and wives. My husband then told him that this man was like a husband to my son; that Rick was gay and that he would not attend the wedding unless his lover was invited. My husband also told my brother that our entire family would not attend unless Rick attended. My brother agreed and said it was perfectly all right with him.

Richard stressed in his interview with us how important it has been to incorporate Rick's lover, Stuart, into the family and to show members of the extended family the way. "Rick's commitment to Stuart is the underlying reason for our adjusting so well. We truly are a family—all of us—my married sons and their wives and children and Rick and Stuart, in a way that I'm sure has to be unique." Demonstrating how well the family has integrated Rick's lover, Richard noted that both Rick and Stuart baby-sit for the grandchildren. He characterized their integrated familial situation as "strictly utopia," but it was clear that the Steins worked hard to arrive at such a utopia. "I show a love and affection for Stuart as well as for Rick," Richard told us. "They both get a kiss and a hug from me whether there are others around or not."

The case of the Steins, who had initially reacted to Rick's disclosure "in a state of hysteria," demonstrates that parents can change. The benefits of the high level of integration achieved by the Steins are quite remarkable. In contrast to ambivalent and disintegrated families, the lives of parents and their gay or lesbian children in integrated families are as interconnected and vital as they would be if the child were heterosexual. In such families meaning and purpose are no longer derived from conformity to a socially constructed Myth of heterosexual bliss. The parents understand the importance of letting go of that exclusive ideal. The narratives of parents in integrated families described how

courage overcame fear, pride replaced disgrace, and affiliation sup-
planted alienation. These families learned to live and love maturely.
They rightly looked forward to a shared future of rich and diverse-but-
interconnected selves.

The Insidiousness of Disintegration

As we have been suggesting, because homosexuality is stigmatized by
our culture, it becomes a source of shame that promotes fragmentation.
When a child recognizes that he or she is different and understands that
this difference is stigmatized by the society at large and within his or her
own family, the process of disintegration within the family begins. The
child will decide, at least at first, to conceal rather than reveal this difference. Driven largely by fear, the strategies of secrecy, obfuscation, dis-
sembling, distance, and deceit subsequently become tools and devices by
which the inner workings of a family are dismantled. Collusion on the
part of parents and siblings, as we have seen, may further exacerbate the
difficulty of disclosure. As time passes, the shame grows and the silence
of the demilitarized zone is deafening, until one day people give up in
despair, feeling it is "too late" to change the situation.

The parents may not even be aware of what is happening when a gay
or lesbian child gives up on the possibility of family intimacy. Where the
child adopts a strategy of people-pleasing and accommodation, parents
might actually delight in the child's successes as a reflection of the family's "strength." The disintegration of the family actually occurs secretly,
automatically, from within, long before its outward signs are visible. The
child fears that disclosure will disrupt family life and relationships, that
being open is so threatening that he or she may be attacked or even
destroyed. Experiences of harassment, violence, gay-bashing, and
related manifestations of homophobia and heterosexism serve to reinforce these anxieties. Indeed, such fears are not unrealistic, especially in
families in which there is a risk of violence or abandonment.

Regardless, lesbian or gay children conceal not just their sexual orientation but also the feelings associated with this concealment: loneliness, isolation, a desperate desire for support and acceptance restrained
by an equally desperate fear of disappointing others or of being
rejected, humiliated, or abused. They have given up on the development
of the self in the context of the family. Often, by the time parents learn

that their child is gay, many years may have passed—along with missed opportunities and increased alienation. The fragmentation progresses even if the parents fail to recognize it as such. The path toward reintegration is more difficult to discern.

The O'Donnells: A Beautiful Beginning

When parents choose to integrate their child's sexual orientation into their lives, to love and to act, they invariably strengthen the bonds of family and enhance its capacity to respond in healthy and effective ways for all of its members. How does a family get there? How do families of gay and lesbian children address the myriad dilemmas they must face? What does the process of integration look like? We offer the stories of two families from our study that illustrate this process most clearly.

The story of the O'Donnell family is particularly compelling, for it illustrates this process rather dramatically and demonstrates how a child's coming out may not only restore full functioning to a family but also enhance and transform the family. Kathy O'Donnell speaks lovingly of the birth of her son, Jonathan:

> When he was born, I had the easiest time delivering him of the three, and I was awake for the delivery. When they showed him to me, he was smiling and all the nurses said, "What a beautiful baby!" And it was as if he were saying, "Look world, I'm here! Glad to be here!" He was just the sweetest little baby. He would smile and eat and he was precocious; at age three he took an interest in learning to read and I wasn't pushing him. I'm not that kind of mother. . . . He could always entertain himself. He was amazing right off!

Jonathan was distinctly sociable with most people and very outgoing. He excelled in music and dance. Kathy and her husband, Andrew, encouraged Jonathan to develop his gifts. Jonathan became proficient in piano, violin, and dance, and his teachers praised him. He also performed exceptionally well academically.

FRAGMENTATION

Kathy and Andrew's son Michael was two years older than Jonathan, Another son, Steven, was four years younger. The O'Donnell children grew up in a comfortable middle-class suburb of Chicago. Andrew O'Donnell progressed in his career as an accountant, and Kathy focused on the challenge of rearing three boys.

As the years progressed, however, Kathy and Andrew experienced increasing conflict. Slowly, somewhat imperceptibly, their marriage began to deteriorate. Andrew seemed preoccupied and inattentive, and Kathy felt drained and unsupported. Jonathan seemed outwardly unfazed by the trouble that was brewing. At the age of ten he was diagnosed with a congenital heart problem that was treated with moderate success. Steven was subsequently diagnosed with a similar problem that was also successfully treated. When Jonathan was thirteen years old, Kathy's parents and brother all died in the same year. The stress of these events, combined with the Jonathan's medical problems, overwhelmed the family. The various unhappy events all seemed to contribute to the demise of the marriage. By the time Jonathan was fourteen, Kathy and Andrew had separated.

One year later they amicably divorced. Andrew and Kathy agreed to a joint custody arrangement for their offspring and remained in close proximity to each other to minimize the disruption to their children's lives. Michael, seventeen at the time, seemed to have been affected most deeply by the change. Resentful and rebellious, he chafed at his mother's attempts to discipline him and seemed to blame her for the divorce. Finally, Kathy and Andrew agreed that Michael should live with his father and that the two younger boys would continue to live with Kathy. Kathy described the closeness of her new subunit of the family: "When I moved here, the divorce was over and it was the three of us—Jonathan, Steven, and I—and it was really pretty harmonious, and I was so happy we got along so well."

Jonathan remained popular and involved in high school, winning numerous awards for service and performance. Kathy recalled in our interview Jonathan's remarkable ability to adapt to many different types of people, both in school and outside: "He was able to cross over into different age groups and types. . . . He chose friends for a lot of reasons." But he was also perplexing at times, a bit secretive. Kathy explains that he was something of a chameleon, "trying to be what everyone wanted him to be or what he thought everyone wanted him to be."

As for romance in his life, Kathy remarked, "He didn't date. Now mind you, he never missed a prom or a dance; he was often asked as a girl's choice, but it was . . . always pretty platonic. He never wanted to go to any of the mixed parties: he'd shy away from that. You know, in a sense he was almost too good. He was home a lot, studying, writing papers."

Kathy subsequently began a new romantic relationship of her own with Warren, whose presence Jonathan resented. Kathy wondered if Jonathan felt threatened, as if Warren might usurp him in some way. Still, nothing interfered with Jonathan's academic performance. He graduated with a rank of tenth in his class of 530 students. Both Andrew and Kathy were exceedingly proud of their ideal child. He seemed to be quintessentially low-maintenance and trouble-free.

COLLAPSE

Andrew and Kathy felt supremely confident in sending Jonathan off to college. Jonathan had always succeeded. He made friends easily and invariably became quite popular. The ensuing events, therefore, shocked everyone. As Kathy described this stunning turn:

He left for college in August. . . . I didn't hear from him a lot and when I did, it was weird and he was upset. I called him because he was just strange, even when he came home for weekends, which was rare. . . . He was saying he wasn't sure he could stick it out and maybe he wanted to leave. . . . I felt real panicked inside—like he had to get out of there. . . . Then he just broke down sobbing and crying and telling me he was afraid to leave his room. That was when he said he was gay and . . . said he was in a dorm filled with jocks and he knew as he walked down the halls that they looked at him and knew he wasn't right. He was real homophobic, internalizing it all. I think he could no longer contain the facade of being straight and he really had something of a breakdown there, an emotional upheaval. At any rate, he came home. I find it interesting that he chose to live in the dorm that was all sports jocks there. I think that maybe he wanted to believe he was straight; no maybe about it—I know he did. So I really encouraged him to come home. He tried therapy and support while he was at school but I don't think he was in any shape to stay in school. He was very frightened and talked about suicide. He came home the first of November.

What explains this radical turn of events? How could a model child like Jonathan collapse so precipitously?

As we suggested earlier, adolescent development can be different for lesbian and gay teens than it is for heterosexual teens. It is common, for example, for younger lesbians and gay men to develop a repertoire of what may be called "compensatory" and "people-pleasing" behaviors in order to manage and avoid stigmatization. Jonathan's academic and artistic achievements may have served to compensate during high school for an inner sense of failure or inadequacy in areas pertaining to sexual development. His likability and capacity to find camaraderie with so many different types of people may have provided him with a way to overcome the inherent alienation and fear of rejection common to many lesbians and gay males, particularly in adolescence. Perhaps he constructed an array of "false selves," i.e., facades, images, and appearances that served more to conceal than reveal his identity. It is possible that Jonathan even hid his feelings from himself.

Jonathan's compensatory, people-pleasing behavior apparently helped him survive by avoiding the pain of rejection and alienation from peers in high school. Yet the cost to him was the utter rejection of his own self. When he went away to college and found himself in what he believed to be an alien and inhospitable environment, among sports jocks, where his earlier people-pleasing behavior was not effective, he found that he had no "self" to fall back on.

It is difficult for any gay adolescent to come out. The pressures to conform to heterosexual peer culture, replete with heterosexual milestones (first crush, first date, first high school dance, first prom, first heterosexual experience, etc.), are very intense. It takes immense courage to withstand the pressures and keep faith with one's own inner being. Many cannot do it. Additionally, when Jonathan's parents' marriage was deteriorating and his mother was beset with a variety of crises involving sickness and death, the family was burdened. Perhaps in light of these burdens, Jonathan sought to avoid placing still more weight on his parents or disappointing them any further. Kathy hinted at this when she described her relationship with Jonathan: "It's real loving but he feels real responsible and doesn't want to disappoint anyone. He feels maybe too responsible."

We hypothesize that Jonathan long remained the "best little boy," unable to develop and deepen his identity through the complex process of integrating one of the most fundamental aspects of that identity: sexual orientation. His strategy for dealing with his life appears to have left him vulnerable to internal pressures to conform. Like other gay men and lesbians, he may have compromised himself through his desires to please others. While his reaction is understandable, it also short-circuited the more normative adolescent developmental experiences of individuation often characterized by some degree of unpleasantness, rebelliousness, or oppositional behavior.

At college, his strategy shattered, unleashing an explosive mix of Jonathan's pent-up frustrations and his fear of rejection, alienation, and loss. Kathy's account of Jonathan's first months in college depicted a young man desperately struggling to convince himself and others that he is the quintessential heterosexual, sports-oriented male. If others are convinced of this, he seems to have reasoned, perhaps it will in fact be so! Yet it was not long before he felt he could neither convince others nor himself. Jonathan's lack of successful separation and individuation from his familial role apparently exacerbated the problem, rendering him ill-equipped for the experience of being away from home among strangers.

RESPONSE AND INTEGRATION

When Jonathan finally came out, the immediate response from his family was one that will by now be familiar to the reader: a sense of loss, anger, guilt, shame, inadequacy. "You know what my first feeling was?" Kathy remembered, "That he'd never have children; that that is just not going to be, is real hard. And that I just feel like . . . I know the world is a hard place but I won't understand the dangers he'll face." But, Jonathan's coming out also provided the entire family with an opportunity to realign itself in a way that could significantly enhance the well-being of each of its members. His act of disclosure set into motion a series of changes in relationship patterns between family members that allowed the family to move beyond the "closed ranks" arrangement that followed the divorce, to one characterized by differentiation and "letting go."

Despite Kathy's initial response to Jonathan, she offered love and support, just as she had in all the previous family crises: "I told him that I loved him and that whatever I could do for him I would do for him, and that it really didn't matter as long as he was all right and that if he really

couldn't deal with it he should come home and get therapy and whatever." This contrast to the scenes of disintegrated families who attached
strings to their love and support is striking. Kathy, despite her first feelings, understood that she must not turn away from her child at the
moment of his greatest need for renewed affirmation of the bonds of
love.

Kathy described Jonathan's reentry into her home as anything but
harmonious. In fact, it appears that Jonathan's nascent integration of his
sexual orientation required the reworking of those adolescent developmental tasks that were truncated by his earlier fearful response to stigma.
At the age of eighteen he assumed the typical adolescent role:

> I was seeing a part of him that I didn't see or know before, or allow
> myself to see before. Instead of a loving, pretty well-balanced, stable
> child, I was seeing a mixed-up, scared, irritable person. He was real
> reckless for a couple of months and I was really very, very angry. He
> started at Horizons [the program for lesbian and gay youth in
> Chicago]. He'd be gone all night or two days in a row and I didn't
> know where he was. I was at the end of my rope and I said to him "I
> know you think you're worldly-wise and want to find out who you
> are but we live in a dangerous world and it isn't as easy as in litera-
> ture." And I really did confront him with that if he kept living this
> way and didn't respect my feelings and worrying about him, that he
> couldn't live here. . . . So, it was a real roller coaster!

How were she and Jonathan able to work through that difficult
phase? Most of all, Kathy recounted her own process of "letting go."
Through Jonathan's coming out, she faced the limits of her ability to
secure the well-being of her children. She recognized that she could not
control their destiny. Equally important, she confronted the possibility
that her own sense of meaning and purpose in life could not be derived
solely from the accomplishments of her children. This admission to herself was especially critical to her relationship with Jonathan, from whose
accomplishments she had derived such great satisfaction. At various
points in the interview Kathy amply demonstrated this process of realization and change:

> Jonathan felt maybe it was given to him by me and his father that he's
> the star and now he's fallen. . . . I've told him that's my problem and
> that's not his problem. You know the old adage, "You live through

your children"? Well, I've had to learn to let go. I kind of basked in the light of his achievements before. Now, I just want him to be happy and okay. We've all had to learn to separate. And that's painful. Obviously, I've had trouble with separation myself. . . . Their father may have as great or greater problem with separation. I feel as though I have to come to terms with the dangers he faces, but they're his, not mine. I think that's the hardest thing I've ever had to do. It's hard to think I can't protect him from all these hurts . . . nor can I protect my straight children either.

It was not easy for Kathy to deal with her own ambivalent feelings toward Jonathan's new-found independence. But now she compared Jonathan's behavior and her reactions before his coming out and since, realizing:

When I would come home from work [then], every night he'd be sitting there doing work, and there are times now when I come home and he's not sitting there and I think, well, that's good, he should be out! I think that he's more himself now. It's like, "Will the real Jonathan stand up?!" and he has, and there's something wonderful about that!

The effect of Jonathan's coming out on Steven, the younger brother, was not uncomplicated. Steven, as the brother of a gay man, felt himself victimized by society's homophobia, and he was not happy about that. He saw Jonathan as culpable. Because Jonathan came out not just to family but also to neighborhood friends, Steven complained that he had to contend at school with taunting from peers, not because of anything he did or who he was but solely because he had a gay brother. Steven, at the point of the interview, could not see the injustice of blaming the victim. Kathy said that Steven became distraught and demanded of her: "I want him to be out of here, gone, get rid of him!" Kathy was clearly upset by Steven's distress, yet she was hopeful that eventually Steven would come to appreciate his brother's bravery and honesty, and out of that appreciation a new and more mature sibling relationship could form.

Kathy found it difficult to describe her ex-husband's reactions to Jonathan's disclosure. Within one week of Jonathan's coming out to her, she had called Andrew to convey the information to him. Interestingly, she regretted having done this, thinking soon after she did it that the decision should have been Jonathan's. She believed, however, that

Jonathan was "far more afraid of his father's reaction," and so, perhaps, she sought to intervene and thereby protect him.

Andrew expressed to Kathy some fear of "losing" Jonathan; he also appeared to regard Jonathan's homosexuality as just "a phase." Perhaps he blamed himself, as well. In any case, Kathy observed that Jonathan and his father had never been very close, but despite Andrew's ambivalence, they now—once Jonathan's "secret" was out—"tried" to understand and accept each other better. She felt that there was at least some promise in this effort toward a closer bond between them.

The reaction of Warren, Kathy's boyfriend, was helpful to both Kathy and the rest of the family. Warren may have had some notion prior to Jonathan's coming out that Jonathan might be gay. Kathy confided the news to Warren a day or two after Jonathan had told her. His reaction "was real wonderful, you know? It was so nice. He said, 'That kid's got a lot of guts. It takes a lot to get it out.' "

There was thus a shift in Jonathan's relationship to Warren. Kathy recalled: "Jonathan's reaction at first [on meeting Warren] was like he couldn't even be in the same room with him, but he was polite. And from that has grown a real genuine caring. I can see that Jonathan is happy that I have someone in my life that I love, and he likes Warren."

Perhaps Warren's new-found respect for Jonathan has earned Jonathan's warm response. However, one might also speculate that Jonathan has "let go" as well. He has relinquished his own internalized sense of excessive responsibility for his mother's well-being, allowing Warren to fulfill his appropriate role in Kathy's life.

As a result of Jonathan's coming out, the postdivorce alignments that, like a logjam, had blocked the flow of change and growth for the whole family, were dislodged. As difficult as the situation was at the time, the "Kathy-Jonathan-Steven" axis became more differentiated. Kathy commented, "This has created new ways of looking at things and adjusting. We've all had to learn to separate, and that's painful." Jonathan and his older brother, Michael, began to form a new relationship as well: "Jonathan isn't passive anymore. Michael has always been sort of the brute and Jonathan isn't allowing it anymore," Kathy observed. Once Jonathan claimed himself, a more equal distribution of power between siblings began to become possible.

The transformative and "corrective" power of coming out is evident in the lives of the O'Donnells, who had been frozen in a postdivorce configuration. The adolescent developmental process was unleashed for Jonathan. His personality became more integrated both internally and (in relationship to his family, neighbors, and friends) externally. Jonathan's coming out also allowed the rest of the family to redefine itself. Jonathan, his mother, and his brother Michael were all freed from a constrictive set of expectations and roles. While it remained to be seen how Steven would handle the homophobia that he learned from his peers, and while we had no way of anticipating the O'Donnells' future, at the time of the interview much that was constructive had already been engendered by Jonathan's act of self-disclosure. Progress, while not certain, was likely. As Kathy O'Donnell concluded, "Seeing my children as separate from me, people who make their own choices, that's been a tremendously positive thing here; on the positive side, that's probably been the greatest."

The Jarrett Family—Finding the Missing Piece

The Jarretts too came a long distance in a short time. At the time of our interview they had arrived at a place where they accepted their son's homosexuality and felt that they could also appreciate that it made some contribution to their own lives. Matt Jarrett, a minister, and his wife, Susan, had felt that they had reason to worry about their younger son, Kurt, from his early childhood. Born with a birth defect that, while not disfiguring, mildly affected his coordination and his speech, Kurt faced numerous difficulties throughout childhood. Matt and Susan could cope with the medical aspects. What they found much more difficult to cope with, however, was Kurt's unhappy relationships with his peers. The speech and coordination problems became a focus of taunting from other children. Matt and Susan tried always to encourage Kurt and instill in him pride and self-esteem, along with their own strong faith that their religion afforded them. But they felt frustrated and helpless as they watched him isolate himself.

The Jarretts had another son, Eric, five years older than Kurt, who, according to Susan, had always made friends easily. He was something of a "golden boy"—easy-going, successful, and affable. As Susan described Eric: "Maybe if our first son hadn't been so popular, the contrast between him and Kurt wouldn't have been so great; but it was like night and day!" Kurt was always wary of children his own age. As Susan explained, "He really did not bond well with his peers. So for a lot of years it was really just the three of us [Matt, Susan, and Kurt]." In fact, Kurt's dependence on his parents and inability to separate became so problematic that at one point they sought counseling, which Susan recalled as being only moderately helpful. Kurt did fairly well academically in high school, but he continued to insulate himself from rejection by closely involving himself with his parents. Matt and Susan, in the meantime, prided themselves on the open communication and closeness in their family, which continued until Kurt completed high school.

Kurt chose to live at home while going to a nearby college. College precipitated a crisis for him, just as it had for the O'Donnell's son Jonathan. Kurt's grades plummeted, and he changed schools. His parents were perplexed about this sudden academic nosedive. It was then that Kurt confided to his father that he thought he might be gay. Matt dismissed the confidence, responding, "Well, we all fall somewhere on a scale, but don't label yourself until you know for sure." However, he was also quick to add, "I don't think you're gay," and as Kurt requested, he told no one about their discussion.

When Kurt was a college junior, Matt took a position in another city—which meant that for the first time, Kurt would be on his own. Matt and Susan moved away. Kurt began to live in a dorm. Susan commented, "I think before he kind of used us as his social contact. Our move forced Kurt to get out of it more and take care of himself."

So he did. Kurt began to acknowledge his sexual orientation more fully and sought out the campus gay group for support. Susan observed:

> I don't think he would have done this if we'd been there. I think it forced him to look at himself. We were kind of his basic support system and when that was gone, he tried to look into himself more and figure himself out. In May he came down on the train and we went out to dinner to a Mexican restaurant—I'll never forget it. He just kind of blurted it out over the meal. I don't know why but it didn't particularly surprise me. He felt so proud of himself: it was like he was telling us something wonderful had happened, so I couldn't feel bad. And then he pulled out a picture of a young man. On the back this man had written a very touching statement of friendship for Kurt. All through the years I had just waited for him to show me a picture of a young woman. I just gave him a big hug and said, "I'm so happy for you," and I was because he had finally found someone he

could care about, who cared about him. It wasn't a young lady, which I had secretly hoped for all these years, but because he seemed so generally pleased and happy, my initial reaction—it was okay. So that was just last May—not very long ago. Obviously, he had done his homework in that group. He told us they had spent a lot of time talking about how to come out to your parents.

Susan revealed in the interview not only her relief that her son had finally found some joy and comfort in his life but also her relief that what had perplexed her before was now clear:

> It was like it was the missing piece of a puzzle for me. It answered a lot of questions for me about Kurt's inability to form close relationships with young girls, and with boys, too. These feelings must have been within him for a long time and made him awkward and unnatural with his peers. It was kind of that missing piece of the puzzle; it kind of told me why he was with us so much. We were safe and accepting and obviously he'd been wrestling with this for years and I could sense within him that relief. He too had found that missing piece of his life. He seemed so happy and he does to this day seem so much happier.

Susan emphasized that she felt a sense of genuine hope about her son for perhaps the first time:

> I've always been so concerned about him because of his medical problems and his inability to form close relationships with his peers. It's almost like now I could feel, "Okay, he can go and live now." It was almost a celebration, although I know that's naive. I know it's going to be hard for him, but at least everything is out on the table.

Her relief and hope were tinged with anguish, at least in part because of her realization of the difficulties that a homophobic society would be likely to impose on her son. She knew she must find support to help her deal with this anguish.

Her husband, Matt, also needed support. Matt was able to work his way out of the panic he had felt at Kurt's first disclosure, when Kurt was a freshman. But Matt, like his wife, was not yet entirely comfortable about his son's homosexuality because of his fears about the reactions from a homophobic world. However, he too felt that Kurt's honesty and self-assertion could only be for the good:

> I'm a little more comfortable accepting Kurt the way he is now. As a father, I always wanted him to fit the ideal male image. I was a little uncomfortable with Kurt in public because he didn't act as appropriately as, let's say, Eric. But my discomfort has diminished in recent years, although it's not completely gone. I guess I still have in the back of my mind some ideal for him—which isn't reality. He has really matured. His telling us he's gay has been better for our relationship. He's not so guarded . . . he can be more real. His telling us represents his knowing himself better. My hopes for Kurt's future are brighter now. He's doing very much better academically. He's back on track.

Matt's adjustment did not come easily. Through a counselor he and Susan were referred to Parents, Families, and Friends of Lesbians and Gays (PFLAG). Their willingness to attend a PFLAG meeting demonstrated the kind of "active love" described earlier, which has the potential of generating immense growth. Susan recalled the drama of her first PFLAG meeting:

> It was very difficult sitting in a large circle, going around introducing ourselves, and I just couldn't talk. I said our name and then I started to say "Our son is gay" and then I just broke down and wept— because I had never said that out loud, let alone to a group of strangers—that was really hard.

Despite the initial discomfort that both Matt and Susan experienced, they declared in our interview that they derived immense benefit from their PFLAG experience. For Susan, the best aspect of it was "the understanding of that community of what I'm going through as the parent of a gay child and everything that means. The common bond. . . . So far, it's all just been positive. As we get on in all of this, I suppose there'll be some things lacking, but right now it's all still so new that we're just lapping it up, so to speak."

They continued to worry about their son, but the worry focused on a set of milestones that they could anticipate. As Susan explained:

> We talk about what it means for Kurt and his life and what it will mean for us as he becomes more open with other people, and things we're afraid of—what will people think in the church? We're just barely

able to talk about what it will mean for Kurt when he gets into a relationship, and how that will affect us. It's one thing saying we accept it and another now to actually live that out. But I trust that will happen. We are trying to become more comfortable with the fact of it ourselves personally, by reading, by getting to know the gay community better. By becoming more familiar with what all this means, so that when we are open as parents, we'll be open out of strength, not weepy or wishy-washy, so that we'll be well-grounded emotionally and intellectually. I don't know if that will ever happen, but I hope it will.

Susan agreed also that Kurt's coming out has brought her and her husband closer together. As she described it, "I feel more intimacy. I guess it's because it's another thing we've gone through together."

Susan had always been puzzled by the differences between her two sons, but she now saw those differences in a new light. She was grateful that Eric responded well to Kurt's disclosure, that he had always stood solidly in life and the news did not shake him. But she was especially touched that Kurt had finally come in to his own, and that he now claimed his strength in a very real sense, even becoming her teacher:

Kurt seems just years ahead of his older brother in terms of self-understanding because he's had to do some work that other young people haven't had to do. Eric is kind of the perfect kid, so I don't feel like I've learned so much from him. I love him, but it's kind of through Kurt's struggles the I've become a more complete person. As a young parent, when Kurt was having so many problems with relationships (which I had never had), it sort of perked my awareness of the "loner," the isolated person, people who aren't part of the "in" group. It's made me a more tolerant person. I've been learning from Kurt my whole adult life and this is kind of just another opportunity.

She concluded with a metaphor in which we found wisdom and love: "Eric was always a flower and Kurt was like a seed that turned into a flower garden. Eric was always fine, but Kurt was always up for grabs because of this physical problem. And then he just transcended it. He became a flower garden. He just really blossomed!"

6

You Have Something to Hear

New Cultural Ideals

When parents choose to integrate their gay or lesbian child fully into their lives, they commit an act of love and heroism. For the love of their child, they challenge their friends, family, and neighbors. They confront an array of cultural institutions and centuries of social history that would consign them and their child to ignominy. Each step toward integration helps to move our culture away from the *universal* imperative of an ideal that oppresses lesbians, gay men, and their families because it shames them.

A Brief History of the Stigmatizing of Homosexuality

The social history of homosexuality can be traced now due to the efforts of a new generation of historians, sociologists, and anthropologists who have discovered a complex story about same-sex relations in culture and society.[1] As these scholars have shown, homophobia evolved through the ages. Homosexuality was deemed at some points in time a sin, at other points "moral degeneracy," at others a "disease," and now, more recently, a "destructive lifestyle" or a "genetic flaw." Each classification or attribution continued to promote the stigmatization of same-sex love. But all these negative terms reflect more myth than science or moral profundity. They are the signs of a shame culture and a history that assigns blame for being lesbian or gay. The historical attempts to classify, categorize, morbidify, criminalize, and condemn love between women or love between men also reflect a culture's wish to validate a central organizing principle for all human relationships. But that principle is no longer relevant to everyone, nor is it necessary in order for society to thrive that the principle be universally followed.

The Church's aim to stigmatize homosexuality, as scholars have argued, grew out of the politics and ascetic movements of its early history and an over-riding emphasis on the promotion of procreation. With the Enlightenment, medical science began to supplant religion in Western culture. Though the Enlightenment valorized rationality, sexual deviance continued to be treated harshly, even by execution. It is within the context of scientific study and the classification of sexual differences that the identity of "the homosexual" eventually emerged, during the second half of the nineteenth century.

Nineteenth- and early twentieth-century medical men, such as Richard von Krafft-Ebing, Havelock Ellis, and Sigmund Freud, attempted to lessen antihomosexual prejudices by explaining homosexuality as a medical rather than a moral problem. But their well-intentioned efforts were in the end very destructive. This line of thinking was to allow the Nazis, later in the twentieth century, to condemn and murder homosexuals as "diseased." And for a very long time in the twentieth century, many authorities, including those who were compassionate and did not believe that homosexuality merited imprisonment or punishment, nevertheless continued to view it as an innate sickness that required treatment.[2]

Scientific sexology was divided over these theories in the first half of the twentieth century. Freud, for instance, early in his career, developed a "degeneration" theory about homosexuality. More than thirty years later, however, in his famous 1935 letter to an American mother, Freud suggested that homosexuality was "no vice, no degradation [and] cannot be classified as an illness." Freud argued that homosexuality, like left-handedness, could probably not be changed and should be accepted by the homosexual and his family.

However, by the 1940s a number of American psychiatrists sought to reinstate the "disease model," arguing that homosexuality was caused by bad parenting. For many years, psychoanalytic study continued to perpetuate this false idea.[3] Homosexuality was labeled a mental illness, a point of view that flourished in mid-twentieth-century America, particularly during the 1950s when the pressure of Cold War toward conformity was at its height. The homosexual became a key target for blackmail and arrest, an object of scorn, and was even associated with communism and traitorous conduct. Raids on gay bars and even gay people's private parties were common. Scandal was frequent, since people arrested as homosexuals often had their names published in the newspapers. Mistrust was high and secrecy seemed tantamount to survival.

It is against this backdrop that the first real challenges to heterosexual orthodoxy and homosexual secrecy emerged. First came the Kinsey

Reports, which documented that homosexual behavior was far more common in the United States than had previously been believed. In addition, anthropological studies began to reveal that many societies permit the expression of same-sex desire, often in childhood and adolescence, and that some extend the approval of same-sex relations into adulthood.[4] In the early 1950s, for example, sociologist Clelland Ford and biologist Frank Beach[5] showed that sexual practice varied enormously across a sample of many societies around the world. Homosexual practice was approved and permitted for some persons in more than 60 percent of the groups they surveyed. Shortly thereafter, the great American psychologist Evelyn Hooker[6] offered a critique of existing research on homosexuality as a disease. Hooker interviewed numerous self-identified homosexual men and showed that homosexuals who were not in clinical treatment for emotional problems had no greater incidence of psychological impairment or disturbed relations than their heterosexual counterparts. She also suggested that the stigmatizing of homosexuality was far more harmful to the psychological well-being of gay men than any aspect of homosexuality itself.

In addition, with the introduction of widespread birth control and the emergence of the sexual liberation movement in the 1960s, the absolute link between sex and procreation was broken. If sex between a man and a woman could be viewed primarily as a form of human expression and source of pleasure rather than being exclusively the means to reproduction of the species, then justice demanded that the prejudice against same-sex relationships be questioned. The civil rights struggles and the women's liberation movement in the 1960s also influenced a new and more humanistic psychology that looked seriously at the problems of power, oppression, discrimination, and abuse in society. Gays and lesbians in the 1960s and 1970s increasingly came to see themselves as an oppressed group and began to challenge actively the notion of homosexuality as a mental illness, a sin, or a crime.

The famous Stonewall Inn riots in New York in 1969, now celebrated every June through the commemoration of the Gay and Lesbian Pride Day Parade, was a watershed. The riots took place on a sultry summer evening, when a typical police raid on a homosexual tavern did not lead to the usual intimidation or slinking away: instead, homosexuals fought back. The Stonewall riots marked the symbolic beginning of a long movement to end discrimination based upon sexual orientation.

A new American culture-formation of individual development began to distinguish between the identity constructs of "homosexual" and those of "gay" or "lesbian."[7] The gay and lesbian rights movement largely rejected the term "homosexual," which was created in the nineteenth century under the influence of the disease model and (1970s militants argued) resulted in feelings of secrecy and shame. The terms "gay" and "lesbian" were more widely adopted and fostered pride and dignity. David Leavitt's novel *The Lost Language of Cranes* eloquently captures the difference between the pre- and post-Stonewall generations. Leavitt presents a closeted homosexual father, who fears the shame of his desires and blames himself for the failure of his marriage, and his openly gay son, who takes pride in his aspirations, including the desire to have a lover and be open to his parents.

Sweeping cultural change and more empirically sound research soon made it apparent that the notion of homosexuality as "illness" has no basis in science, and that the notion's only purpose was to perpetuate stigmatizing myths. In 1974 the American Psychiatric Association officially declassified homosexuality as a mental illness. Since then scholars and mental health professionals have, by-and-large, understood lesbian and gay lifeways as alternative paths of human development.[8] Many religious groups are trying to overcome homosexuality's stigmatized history in a variety of ways, such as the sanctioning of same-sex marriage and the ordination of gay and lesbian clergy. In spite of this progress, however, discrimination against homosexuals remains legal in many places in the land. Indeed, about twenty states of the United States continue to sanction "sodomy" laws and other forms of legal prohibition of homosexuality.

Eliminating Shame-Based Thinking

In light of the history of homophobia, it is perhaps easy to understand why the vestiges of what we call the "shame-based" approaches to homosexuality continue to permeate our culture in general, and the thinking of many parents in particular. In her book, *Parents Matter*, Ann Muller speaks cogently of the shame that many parents still feel upon hearing the news that their child is gay. She has tried to analyze why parents often feel blamed—by society, by their families, and by themselves. Her insight reminds us of the negative effects of antiquated notions about homosexuality on parents who are grappling with accepting the news of their child's sexual orientation:

> The pathologic view of parents as the cause of homosexuality is still widely believed. Freud's dominant mother and weak father have become a pervasive part of our culture, the trolls of psychiatry. The very imprecision of the Freudian and neo-Freudian categories of parental guilt encourages their continued application. The theory allows the unsophisticated to feel smug, to play doctor. It makes the parents of young children nervous and self-conscious. How much love is enough love? It allows lesbian daughters and gay sons to blame their parents. It creates massive guilt, emotional pain, and self-imposed isolation from parents.

The "reparative therapy" approaches, which claim to convert homosexual people into heterosexuals, represent another attempt of pseudoscience, under the cloak of medical authority, to demean lesbians, gay men, and their families. As researcher Timothy Murphy concludes in his review of attempts to redirect sexual orientation, "there would be no reorientation techniques where there was no interpretation that homoeroticism is an inferior state."[9] Clearly the heroic struggle that parents and their gay and lesbian children face is to confront these remnants of an earlier era, acknowledge their destructive impact, and develop a new set of cultural ideals more suitable to the reality of who they are and what they require to build meaningful lives.

Loving Through Action: The Carlsons

In our study we were fortunate to encounter parents who committed themselves to just such heroic labors. In one case, through a series of courageous steps, a family confronted and perhaps transformed the central institution in their lives—their church. Ann and Joseph Carlson, who were seventy-one and seventy-three years old respectively, had been married for more than forty-seven years. They had six children, and their son Mark, the third child, was thirty-nine years old and gay. In Ann's eyes her marriage was a blessing, as she told us, and she and her husband continued to feel blessed, even in their retirement years.

When Mark disclosed to his parents some ten years before our interview that he was gay, the reaction of his father, according to Ann, was "positive and relieved." Joseph had long wondered if his son was homosexual but he did not want to pry into his life. They "did not want to probe," Ann said, because they are "not the kind of people to ask about sexuality." Both Joseph and Ann believed that it was a hopeful sign that Mark would bring up the issue at last, since for many years they had harbored worry and speculation about the hidden areas of Mark's life. Mark chose to disclose his homosexuality by writing a letter to his parents. "That night I read the letter and then Joseph did. We had none of that attitude, 'I don't know but he's not our son' stuff. Some children even swear one parent to secrecy. I couldn't live like that," Ann told us.

At the time Ann and Joseph were both very active in the United Methodist Church, where they were lay ministers. Ann remembered:

> We needed to share [the news of Mark's coming out] with somebody. We needed information. Because of our connection with the church, it seemed the logical place to go. We'd been told all our lives that pastors do that. He responded lovingly. Not judgmental. He listened. Assured us we weren't the only people in the world with a gay son. I think he himself still has trouble with the subject. It's such a political football in the Methodist Church. He doesn't have any problem with homosexuals, but he doesn't want them ordained. . . . We were in the mood for telling people anyway. We were not about to keep our child hidden. Talking to our pastor reinforced our ability to tell others. After we got Mark's letter, the next Sunday, Joseph was supposed to lead our church study group in a discussion of homosexuality. [This was coincidence, she said.] But we decided not to tell the group about Mark's letter. However, at that next meeting, a woman who'd been at the previous meeting said if her son was gay, she'd pray about him, and love him— until he changed! I said, "Now—Mona, he won't change." Then I told the group that Joseph had something to say. [Ann said that she did this spontaneously, and Joseph was surprised but agreed to go on.] We told them, and you could hear a pin drop. Total silence. One dear old woman, she's ninety now, said it did not matter, she still loved Mark. Another man squeezed me on the shoulder . . . his son had all the earmarks of being gay—lived with another man for years.

This was the beginning of many discussions about homosexuality in the congregation, as Ann told us:

A year later, Joseph was a delegate to the Methodist conference, and there was a family resolution that would be very detrimental to lesbians and gays. He stood up and said he had children and that the motion would hurt them. He was very emotional. It was very early in our coming out process. Other people were sympathetic and got to the microphone and the motion was tabled. People told Joseph he did more good by putting family and faces to the gay issue.

When Ann told the last part of her story, it was clear how proud she was of her husband and the role he had played in opposing prejudice. Indeed, she had reason to be proud. Not only had they successfully negotiated the difficult process of accepting their son's homosexuality, but they had made use of their church as a means of support and a means to come out themselves. And they were taking a part in changing society through the church. Ann also noted how these pursuits and others involving advocacy for their gay son "deepened" her relationship with her spouse.

It is not our intention to argue here that the only approach to integrating a gay or lesbian child successfully is to take public stands at every opportunity. But we do maintain that, as families become more integrated, it becomes increasingly difficult for them not to want to confront displays of homophobia and heterosexism. One's consciousness of the effects of homophobia is heightened by having to deal with them in personal ways: therefore, when the child one loves is hurt by ignorant cultural prejudices, it is hard not to want to combat homophobia. Parents who can do this find new and positive meaning in their child's disclosure. To challenge homophobia is to challenge the forces that make a social and cultural exile of the beloved gay or lesbian child and endanger the relationship between lesbian and gay children and their parents. The loving parents of a gay or lesbian child may even find it impossible to keep silent when encountering the dehumanizing forces that are unleashed by homophobia, whether they be manifested in discriminatory religious policies that fail to uphold "the family"—*their* family—or discriminatory laws that threaten to harm their gay or lesbian child.

Something to Hear

We, the authors of this book (two gay men) are not parents of lesbian or gay children, but our research entailed our talking to scores of such parents. We wish to end this book with a discussion about what we believe those parents who have successfully integrated their lesbian or gay children into their families would want you, our readers, to hear. Our "advice" to you for achieving successful integration derives first and foremost from what these parents have observed and reported to us.

If your child has recently disclosed his or her sexual orientation to you, try to understand the motivation. More often than not, your child wants to include you in his or her life more fully than before. He or she has acted courageously in telling you what has been secret and very difficult to reveal. That act alone is worthy of your respect. Your child's disclosure to you may well be a sign that he or she is feeling more confident, as well as more loving, than ever. Take comfort in such positive development.

Though you may have the wisdom of years regarding many life experiences, understand that your child knows more than you do about what it means to be lesbian or gay. He or she has probably already met or become friends with many more lesbian or gay people, read more, been exposed to more information and become more involved in the gay and lesbian community than you have had either the opportunity or the desire to do. Lesbians and gays have generally had a chance to separate myth from reality and have a fuller understanding of the process of coming to terms with all of this. A gay or lesbian child can be a vital resource to you now, especially as you weigh the impact of disclosing to others that you are the parent of a gay or lesbian child.

The issues you face after the child's disclosure are quite new, to be sure, but consider how you have faced other challenges in the past. What principles guided you in the past toward a successful outcome? Who was there for you? How did you and others in your family operate to ensure that the crisis could be met? You may find in those experiences a way of approaching this challenge and clues for taking positive action.

Find and access the most useful resources for both information and support. Surely the best resource is Parents, Families and Friends of Lesbians and Gays (PFLAG), whose website, (www.pflag.org) can guide you to your local PFLAG chapters, as well as to articles, books, pamphlets, and even other relevant websites. Consider also local gay newspapers, gay groups on nearby college campuses, local gay helplines, and other gay organizations in your community as possible sources of information. (See also appendix 3.)

In a society that is condemning of homosexuality and gay and lesbian people, it can be particularly useful to access family counselors, psychotherapists, or clergy who are knowledgeable about these issues and sympathetic to your needs. Helping professionals who understand the issues that have been presented here can assist your family in progressing through these phases with greater comfort. They can also help to guide you to additional resources and to facilitate dialogue within your family. While psychotherapy and counseling involve significant time, money, and effort, and cannot solve all problems, many have found these sources of support from sympathetic and informed mental health professionals extremely valuable, and we endorse them too.

Talking with other parents of lesbians and gay men is invaluable. Though there were some parents in our study who were too fearful to do so, many of them found talking with other parents to be particularly rewarding in helping them to feel that they are not alone, that they have no reason to feel shame or guilt, and that there are others who understand them. Some parents who are too embarrassed by their confused reactions to share them fully with their children can find great comfort in sharing them with other parents who "have been there." Those other parents, who have gone through similar experiences, can also help the floundering parent address problems that emerge along the way and serve as role models. Again, PFLAG meetings can be the best place to start, though other supports can also be critical.

In fact, it appeared to be particularly important for families to identify a "first tier" of individuals in their lives who were likely to be supportive. Brothers and sisters, friends at work, even grandparents, can sometimes be a source of comfort and reassurance. Disclosure (whether by the gay or lesbian child to the parents or by the parents to others) is best when it represents an invitation to another to become more a part of your life. Consider those you would like to have closer to you now and bring them into your circle of support and confidence.

Collaborate in determining who should be told, when, and how. The families we interviewed who were the most successfully integrated shared a common understanding of the value of "coming out," but they didn't necessarily start out that way. Rather, parents spoke with each other and with their children about the various choices surrounding disclosure and arrived at an understanding over time.

At all times consider the costs of secrecy to you, your gay or lesbian child, and to your relationship with them. Any time you—or your spouse or your child—choose to conceal sexual orientation, you may be setting a pattern that prohibits further integration. When you choose to conceal your child's sexual orientation from those closest to you, you may preclude the integration of other vital aspects of your child's life, such as his or her primary relationship. Should you still choose not to disclose, whether it be out of fear, discomfort, or unpreparedness, be sure to discuss with others that you trust the potential effects of this decision and acknowledge the feelings associated with it. In time you might also want to review your decisions on this matter, much as you would check from time to time the wisdom of other major decisions in your life. Perhaps the reasons that once made secrecy seem so necessary to you have ceased to exist.

Get to know other lesbian and gay people. As you move beyond your own stereotypes, you can see your own child more clearly and love her or him more fully. As you see the variety of lesbians and gay men and the lives they lead, you can begin to envision a good future for your own child and to provide support toward its attainment. But, as the most integrated families learned, you can also begin to let go—to allow your role as parent to recede a bit as you see another child successfully launched into a rapidly changing world. You can make a commitment to be there when needed, but you are free to pursue other aspects of your own identity. In so doing, you can form a new connection with your child as two adults experiencing the excitement and pleasure of learning and growing anew.

Integration is a process, not an event. It will take time. To borrow the words of the great civil rights motto, "Keep your eyes on the prize!" The goal in this entire endeavor of integrating your lesbian or gay child into the family is to strengthen the family and make it whole.

One way that a family manifests its strength is by manifesting through action the love they have for one another. That action may be merely personal (e.g., advocating for your child with other family members so that his or her life partner will be included in extended family events, acknowledging their anniversaries, speaking up when a colleague makes a disparaging remark, welcoming the family of your child's partner). Or it may be more political (e.g., promoting change in the policies of your school or church, or contributing time or money to PFLAG or other worthwhile organizations). In all of these ways you manifest your willingness to act on you love for your child.

Based on what we learned from the interviews, we also offer a series of questions to ask yourself as you become more conscious of the choices that you may have before you as a parent. These are the questions we believe the most integrated of families have, in one form or another, learned to ask themselves. Central to them is the question, How are my actions regarding my gay or lesbian child different from what they would be if he or she were heterosexual?

- Am I less inclined to share information about my child with friends and family for fear of having to disclose the child's sexual orientation?
- Am I less willing to extend myself to my child's partner or the partner's family than I would be if they were a heterosexual couple?
- Am I more hesitant to confront a homophobic remark than I would be to confront one that is racist or anti-Semitic?
- Do I ask less about my lesbian or gay child's life for fear of encouraging her or him to be homosexual?
- Do I offer less to my gay or lesbian child than I would to my heterosexual child because I view the gay or lesbian child as less worthy or entitled?
- Do I allow a greater distance to come between me and my gay or lesbian child than I would if my child were heterosexual?
- Do I sacrifice the well-being of my lesbian or gay child in conformity to cultural standards that may no longer hold relevance and meaning to my life or the life of that child? Do I take the path of least resistance for the sake of timidity or comfort?

These are difficult questions, to be sure: yet they probably mirror the questions that millions of lesbians and gay men must ask themselves every day. The courage it takes to answer these questions honestly may well set families on the path to overcoming unexamined cultural prejudices.

New Cultural Ideals to Sustain a National Family

We are grateful to the families that opened their lives to us. Through their examples and their remarkable stories, we have learned a variety of lessons. Most impressive of all, we have seen many of these families formulate new ideals that we believe have much to offer to our rapidly changing society. These new cultural ideals build on those values of family, love, tolerance, respect, sacrifice, spirit, and commitment that we all hold dear.

Predominant in these ideals must surely be the precept that healthy, functioning families, in all their combinations and permutations, are essential for social well-being. This is true for us as individuals, as well as for our democracy. To the extent that families provide abundant love, respect, and tolerance to their individual members, those members can thrive and society can prosper from all their vital contributions. When families allow shame and stigma to overcome them, the resources they need to thrive are greatly diminished or even lost, and the very unit that holds our society together—the family—unravels.

The families we interviewed who were most successful in integrating their lesbian or gay children recognize same-sex relationships as a normal variation of intimate partnership and family formation. They understand that the relationship between two men or two women carries within it all of the potential for love, kindness, care, sacrifice, and commitment that we associate with the relationship between a man and a woman. When families act courageously by integrating their gay children and their partners, they help those children to realize that potential, and our society is better off for it.

Parents of integrated families have discerned that personal meaning in this time of the new millennium need not be derived solely from the fulfillment of a heterosexual lifecourse. Indeed, as the Steins, the Jarretts, the O'Donnells, the Carlsons, and others so amply demonstrate, a great sense of purpose and meaning in life can come from fostering tolerance and understanding for diversity, beginning with their own family. As these parents worked on recognizing and accepting difference, their view of the world and their place in it expanded.

What better lesson for America—a society challenged as never before by its diversity—than to see families, one by one, accepting and cherishing diversity. We believe that the families we interviewed who were most successful at integration grew to appreciate and value the individuality of their children. It was that growth that permitted them to weave into the fabric of their lives the unique experience of having a gay or lesbian child and to offer their child the assurance of their love and respect. May the example of their growth help our national family find the strength and courage to do the same.

Appendix 1

Tables

The following table shows the level of positive initial response on a scale of 1–6 where 1 is negative and 6 is positive, and the percentage of each category of family who had had some thoughts prior to disclosure that their child might be gay.

Table A1 Initial Responses and Previous Thoughts

	Average initial response of mother	*Average initial response of father*	*Percentage of families who had previously thought their child was gay/lesbian*
Integrated	3.64	3.70	30%
Ambivalent	3.43	2.88	25%
Disintegrated	2.43	1.80	57.1%

Table A2 Levels of Integration by Gender of Child

	Gay Son	*Lesbian Daughter*
Integration	81.8	18.2
Ambivalence	71.4	28.6
Disintegration	57.1	42.9

Specific integration criteria and the percentage of families in each category that met them

Table A3 Criteria for Integration

Family type, percentage	Disintegrated	Ambivalent	Integrated
Reported positive change in relationship between child and mother	11.1	40.9	69.2
Reported positive change in relationship between child and father	14.3	47.6	83.3
Reported positive changes in relationship between parents	37.5	52.4	66.7
Report positive effects on family (closer, more communicative, change in roles)	33.3	60.9	53.8
Acknowledge child's improved state, happiness	22.2	69.6	92.3
Expressed appreciation of positive contribution child's coming out has made to parent's life	66.7	87.7	100
Have disclosed to at least one member of extended family	11.1	78.3	100
Have disclosed to two or more members of extended family	0	60.9	92.3
Have disclosed to at least one friend or coworker	66.7	95.7	100

Table A3 *(continued)*

Family type, percentage	Disintegrated	Ambivalent	Integrated
Have disclosed to two or more friends or coworkers	33.3	87	100
Include lover and/ or "in-laws," even with reservations	0	64.3	100
Include lover and/ or "in-laws," without significant reservations	0	7.7	100
Report involvement in PFLAG or gay/lesbian community	66.7	82.6	100
Can project major life events at least 10 years into child's future	0	40.9	76.9

Appendix 2

*Context and Methods
of the Study*

THIS STUDY WAS THE BRAINCHILD of the late developmental psychologist, Andrew Boxer, who was deeply interested in parent-child relationships, and the family. In collaboration with anthropologist Gilbert Herdt, and later, psychotherapist/social worker Bruce Koff, the study was begun in the late 1980s. As we noted in the introduction, we were able to contact a variety of parents of gays and lesbians who agreed to discuss their experiences of their child's coming out. The interviewers were typically older adults who were themselves heterosexual, gay, and lesbian by orientation, and worked together as a team. The original description and fuller findings and methods of the study are contained in the publications of Boxer et al. (1991), Herdt (1992), and Herdt and Boxer (1993), and we refer the interested reader to these key publications for additional reading. Here we wish to examine the methods of our study.

In our earlier study we examined the changing culture of American homosexuality as constituted through four distinct generations or cohorts (see Herdt and Boxer 1993). Cohort age-differences are likely to have consequences for the study of development in general, and in particular with regard to parent-child relations. Although the oldest living cohort dates from the turn of the century, many of these surviving persons, now in their seventies and older, grew into adulthood and discovered their same-sex desires typically without ever having "come out" to parents or others. Today many of them remain largely invisible. Whereas the oldest cohorts lived in secrecy and with fear, suffering the psychosocial cost, today's youth are developing a future life course by coming out and living gay and lesbian lives (see the short annotated bibliography at the end of appendix 3, for suggestions of further reading to illustrate this theme).

The motivations for and timing of coming out to parents are multi-determined, as this book reveals. They include political and ideological reasons; the need for honesty and the need to reduce the strains of passing or deception; increased confidence and self-esteem resulting from self-acceptance; new personal relationships; anger and confrontation. Disclosure of one's gay/lesbian identity to parents can be a stressful and anxiety-provoking situation for any individual. Few systematic studies have thus far examined the coming out process and its impact on the quality of the parent-child relationship; we have alluded to these throughout the book. Previous investigations, largely based on case reports, portray hiding one's sexual identity from parents as resulting in more distant relationships. Existing data indicate that between approximately 40 to 63 percent of homosexually or gay- and lesbian-identified respondents have reported being open about their sexual orientation to parents (reviewed in Boxer et al. 1991).

The parents in our study (approximately equally divided between fathers and mothers) were recruited from two sources: the parents of youth from the Horizons Community Services agency for gay and lesbian teens in Chicago, and a local social support group for parents with gay and lesbian children. It was primarily because of the youth group that we were able to locate a few parents who were negative or from families we would designate now as "disintegrated." This is perhaps the most difficult family constellation to interview, and few prior studies have seen such parents. The second source of support was the local PFLAG group in Chicago. This group was critical to our recruitment of a broad mainstream. These parents were primarily white, middle- and upper-middle-class, in their fifties, and with young adult sons and daughters who had come out to them, mostly during the children's young adulthood. They were from Protestant, Jewish, and Catholic families. A small number were from minority groups; those parents were also middle-class. They sought social support through membership in the parent group in order to assist them with various aspects of this coming out process. Obviously, our parents were not a random sample; rather, they reflect the constraints of working through voluntary organizations. Consequently, these parents were generally more likely to moving toward integration, as we have indicated earlier in the text. This was also a somewhat older group of parents, as indicated in the text by tables 1 and 2. The length of time since their children had disclosed their homosexuality to them ranged from less than one year to more than ten years. Each father/mother was individually administered a semistructured interview and a battery of paper-and-pencil assessments.

Upon reading the interviews, we arrived at a number of indicators of integration. We then identified key questions, the answers to which served as indicators of integration. Following are the indicators for integration and the corresponding questions we used to elicit information. It should be noted that, because of the narrative nature of the interview, other questions may have at times elicited information relevant to these indicators. Such information was factored into our analysis whenever this occurred. We also realize that some questions did not adequately elicit as much information as we might have liked or to the level of specificity desired. This was particularly true in determining the level of "inclusion." We made allowances for this in our analysis so that families were not rated positively or negatively in respect to integration when information was missing or insufficient.

Indicator 1: Positive changes in relationships between the target child and the parent

A. Describe your relationship with your son/daughter.
B. In general, how would you say things go between you (1=very poor, 2=bad, 3=average, neither good nor bad, 4=good, 5=excellent)?
C. Is that the way your relationship has always been, or would you say that things have changed between the two of you? What is different now? What do you think caused these changes?
D. "How has your child's coming out affected your relationship with your spouse?" (Narrative responses to these changes were subsequently coded to indicate the direction of the change, i.e., better or worse, and the focus of the change, i.e., change in self or change in the child.)

Indicator 2: Expressions of appreciation of positive contribution child's coming out has made to parents life

A. How has learning about your child's sexual orientation affected you as an adult and as a parent? (Probes: How has it affected the way you think of yourself as a parent? How has it affected the way you think of yourself as an individual?)
B. What are the positive things that have happened to you concerning your son/daughter's coming out?

C. What has been the greatest burden regarding your child's coming out? Is there anything you can think of that is upsetting that has happened concerning your child's coming out?

Indicators 3 and 4: Disclosure to others and inclusion

A. Who was the first person you told about your child's sexual orientation? What was your reason for telling them? What was the situation like? How did they respond? Did this experience affect your decision to tell others (or not to tell others)? How? Why not?
B. Do any other members of your family know of your child's sexual orientation? Can you list them for me and tell me how they know of it? Who told them? When were they told? How did they respond?
C. If other family members do not know, is it important to you or to your child that your child's sexual orientation be kept from them? Why is that? Are there family members in particular who you feel must not be told of it? Who? Why?
D. Have you discussed your child's sexual orientation with others outside of the family? Who? What was it like? How did they respond? How did you feel about it? If not, can you tell me about that?

Indicator 5: Positive effect on family

A. How has your child's coming out/being gay affected the relationships in your immediate family? (Probes: Has it brought your family closer together? Has it moved you farther apart? Has it caused changes among relationships within the family? What is the nature of these changes? How did they occur?).

Indicator 6: Acknowledgment of child's improved state

A. Describe your child for me. What is he/she like as a person? How has he/she done in school? (Probe for educational attainments, occupational achievements, etc.)
B. What are the main worries or hassles that you see your child experiencing in her/his life right now?
C. How has your child been helpful/supportive of you in dealing with his/her sexual orientation? Was there anything he/she did that made it more stressful for you?

Indicator 7: Involvement in PFLAG or gay community

A. Have you heard of PFLAG? Have you considered attending? What affects your decision? How long have you been participating in PFLAG?
B. Aside from PFLAG, who was the person, support, or resource that you made most use of in dealing with your son/daughter having come out to you?

Indicator 8: Capacity to project into the future

A. We all think about the future at times, wondering what life has in store for us. We often make guesses or predictions about what might happen in our lives. I would like you to make some guesses now about your son's/daughter's life. What do you expect to happen in his/her life? Tell me as many of these as you can. You don't have to be absolutely certain that what you guess will actually happen. A good guess is good enough. (After each event, interviewer asks: At what age is the event likely to occur?)

Responses to these questions were subsequently analyzed and assigned a value of 1 or 0 based on whether or not such responses indicated integration. These were added to arrive at an aggregate score for integration. Other independent variables were measured against these aggregate scores to determine possible correlation. These variables included age of parent, age of child, degree of religiosity of the parent, educational level, racial/ethnic background, gender of target child, marital status of parent, when told, initial responses, and previous thoughts that the child was gay or lesbian.

We found a propensity for parents to reflect upon the range of issues involving their parenting. The parents raised basic questions, such as, "Who is my child?" and "What do I really want for him/her?" Many of the parents took the opportunity and made the most of it. This was an opportunity for growth and personal development, coincident with their own transitions in middle age and seniority. Some talked about feelings of guilt, not related to the question of causality, but rather because of their initially negative responses to the news that their child was gay or lesbian. This introspective process frequently resulted in a more realistic assessment of parental expectations as well as delineated boundaries between parent and child. Part of this parental self-examination process involved reshaping some of their parental fantasies (Cohen and Weissman, 1984).

Every parent has a set of expectations about their children, including an image of future life events—what those should be and when they should occur. After parents had reoriented themselves to their children's new identity status, they restructured and altered some of their parental expectations regarding the future life course of their children. Through the reciprocal socialization from child to parent (Cook and Cohler 1986), many parents talked about being confronted with the reality of their children's sexual identity in a way they never experienced with their heterosexual children. But more than sexuality, parents talked about the many ways that they became socially and culturally enlightened through the coming out process. Others talked about becoming political activists.

In the earliest study of parents of gays by Ann Muller (1987), the stories of many parents suggested that they became "stuck" in the coming out process at an initial phase. They could not seem to go further. They were able, in essence, to retreat to what Griffin, Wirth, and Wirth (1986) called the "ostrich effect," that is, ignoring their children's homosexuality or pretending that it did not exist. However, the accounts given by those parents who engaged in a high level of denial highlight changes in their acceptance that occurred over time, as well as the differing perceptions of mothers and fathers, in addition to those of sons and daughters. We have also found among our sample of parents that the historical time during which the parents (not the children) began the coming out process affected how they were able to negotiate the process. Just as there are now gay and lesbian adult role models for the youth in our study, so too do parents today find role models to support and facilitate their own coming out process. We wish to emphasize that coming out is a process, not just an outcome. The process of integration in the family context interfaces with the psychosocial interior of the family as a whole, and with the life course trajectories of individual family members. To understand this process more adequately, future researchers must study the whole system across time—even across a generation—to see how psychology and culture are interacting.

SELECTED BIBLIOGRAPHY

Boxer, A. M., J. A. Cook, and G. Herdt. "To Tell or Not to Tell: Patterns of Self-Disclosure to Mothers and Fathers Reported by Gay and Lesbian Youth." In *Parent-Child Relations Across the Lifespan*, ed. K. Pillemer and K. McCartney, pp. 59–93. Oxford University Press, 1991.

Cohen, R. S. and S. Weissman. "The Parenting Alliance." In *Parenthood: A Psychodynamic Perspective*, ed. R. S. Cohen, J. Cohler, and S. Weissman. New York: Guilford, 1984.

Cook, J. and B. J. Cohler. "Reciprocal Socialization and the Care of Offspring with Cancer and with Schizophrenia." In *Life-Span Developmental Psychology: Intergenerational Relations*, ed. N. Datan, A. L. Greene, and H. W. Reese, pp. 223–243. Hillsdale, N.J.: Lawrence Erlbaum, 1986.

Griffin, C. W., M. J. Wirth, and A. G. Wirth. *Beyond Acceptance: Parents of Lesbians and Gays Talk About Their Experiences*. Englewood Cliffs, N.J.: Prentice-Hall, 1986.

Herdt, Gilbert. "Coming Out as a Rite of Passage: A Chicago Study." In *Gay Culture in America*, ed. G. Herdt, pp. 29–67. Boston: Beacon, 1992.

Herdt, Gilbert and Andrew Boxer. *Children of Horizons*. Boston: Beacon, 1993.

Muller, Anne. *Parents Matter*. New York: Naiad, 1987.

Appendix 3

Resources

IT IS OUR HOPE THAT THIS BOOK WILL SERVE to provide some reassurance to parents, families, and helping professionals that there is a path toward wholeness and well-being upon learning that a child is gay or lesbian. We believe that other resources can be helpful as well. A variety of local resources exist within most cities and even small towns and rural areas. If you are unfamiliar with the resources in your area, consider the following steps:

1. Contact PFLAG (see below) to locate the chapter nearest to you and obtain literature and other assistance.
2. Contact the nearest college or university to see if they have a campus organization for lesbian, gay, and bisexual students.
3. Consult a local gay/lesbian newspaper, or other newspapers that may appeal to youth or provide guides to cultural and community events.
4. Contact a local mental health association or center and ask for a referral to a mental health professional who is affirming and knowledgeable about gay and lesbian issues.
5. Contact clergy who you believe will be sympathetic and knowledgeable about gay and lesbian issues.
6. Check out telephone directories, including the Yellow Pages, as well as guides and directories written specifically for the gay/lesbian community that are available in larger cities. (These can be found in book and music stores, clubs, bars, and community centers.)
7. Visit a local bookstore or public library. Some bookstores, including the larger chains, have sections devoted to gay and lesbian issues. On occasion, books on homosexuality are placed (erroneously, we think!) under "gender studies."
8. If you have access to the Internet, consider the following websites, many of which provide links to a vast pool of information on homosexuality, including articles, videos, and on-line discussion groups for parents:

Parents, Families and Friends of Lesbians and Gays:
www.pflag.org
My Child Is Gay! Now What Do I Do?:
www.pe.net/~bidstrup/parents.htm
The SafeTeen Project:
www.gayplace.com/project/project.html
E-Quality's Religion & Homosexuality Links:
www.mrs.umn.edu/~pehng/Equality/religion.html

You may also do an online search and purchase books for parents of lesbians and gays at the websites of major bookstore chains, including Amazon (amazon.com) and Barnes and Noble (barnesandnoble.com).

National Organizations

The following national organizations can be of particular assistance:

1. Parents, Families, and Friends of Lesbians
   and Gays (PFLAG)
   1726 M Street, NW, Suite 400
   Washington, DC 20036
   202–467–8180
   (www.pflag.org.)
2. Human Rights Campaign
   1012 14th St., N.W, #200
   Washington, D.C. 20005
   202–628–4160
   (www.hrusa.org.)
3. Lambda Legal Defense and Education Fund
   202 Wall St., #1500
   New York, NY 10005
   212–809–8585
4. National Center for Lesbian Rights
   870 Market St., #570
   San Francisco, CA 94102
   415–392–6257
   462 Broadway, #500A

New York, NY 10013

212–343–9589

5. National Gay and Lesbian Task Force

2320 17th St. N.W.

Washington, D.C. 20009

202–332–6483

6. National Lesbian and Gay Health Association

1407 S St., N.W.

Washington, D.C. 20009

202–797–3536

7. Gay, Lesbian, and Straight Education Network

122 W. 26th St., #1100

New York, NY 10001

212–721–7652

Additional Reading Resources

While there are few studies of the parents of gays and lesbians, with the exception of the important work of Ann Muller, and Robert A. Bernstein, noted below, several additional books and papers may be of great help to the interested reader wishing to learn more of the general area. We recommend the following texts:

Aarons, Leroy. *Prayers for Bobby: A Mother's Coming to Terms with the Suicide of Her Gay Son.* San Francisco: HarperCollins, 1995.

Ben-Ari, Tirosch Adital. "It's the Telling That Makes the Difference." In R. Josselson and Am Lielich, eds., *Interpreting Experience: The Narrative Study of Lives,* 3: 153–172. Thousand Oaks, Calif.: Sage, 1995.

This is one of the most interesting studies of how gay men and lesbians come out to their families in another culture. The setting is Israel, and through highly rich and sensitive portraits, the author shows the plight of families who experience difficulties with the sexuality of their children.

Bernstein, Robert A. *Straight Parents, Gay Children: Keeping Families Together.* New York: Thunder's Mouth, 1995.

A highly readable personal account of how a father comes to terms with his daughter's homosexuality. The journalist reports on a variety of aspects and problems of being a heterosexual parent of a lesbian or gay child, and makes an impassioned plea for understanding and culture change.

Borhek, Mary V. *Coming Out to Parents: A Two-Way Survival Guide for Lesbians and Gay Men and Their Parents* (rev. and updated). Cleveland, Ohio: Pilgrim, 1993.

Boxer, A. M., J. A. Cook, and G. Herdt. "To Tell or Not to Tell: Patterns of Self-Disclosure to Mothers and Fathers Reported by Gay and Lesbian Youth." In K. Pillemer and K. McCartney, eds., *Parent-Child Relations Across the Lifespan*, pp. 59–93. New York: Oxford University Press, 1991.

This study contains extensive and rich data related to how adolescents who are gay- and lesbian-identified seek to come out and create new identities and relationships with parents and families. This was the first publication of the Chicago Horizons study, which led to Herdt and Boxer's *Children of Horizons* in l993. Highly recommended for detailed analysis of the sociological and clinical patterns.

Cabaj, Robert P. and Terry S. Stein, eds. *Textbook of Homosexuality and Mental Health*. Washington, D.C.: American Psychiatric Association Press, 1996.

The most comprehensive general textbook with a mental health perspective on topics of gay and lesbian mental health available from the leading authorities in the field. While there is no entry on parents of gay men and lesbians, the variety of essays on youth, couples, psychological well-being, and aging are highly useful and recommended for practitioners and general readers alike.

Clark, Don. *Loving Someone Gay* (rev. and updated). Millbrae, Conn.: Celestial Arts Publication, 1987.

Dew, Robb Forman. *The Family Heart: A Memoir of When Our Son Came Out*. New York: Ballantine, 1994.

Fairchild, Betty and Nancy Hayward. *Now That You Know: What Every Parent Should Know About Homosexuality*. New York: Harcourt Brace Jovanovich, 1989.

Griffin, Carolyn Welch, Marian J. Wirth, and Arthur G. Wirth. *Beyond Acceptance: Parents of Lesbians and Gays Tell About Their Experiences* (rev. and updated). New York: St. Martin's Griffin, 1997.

Herdt, Gilbert. "Introduction: Gay Youth, Emergent Identities, and Cultural Scenes at Home and Abroad." In G. Herdt, ed., *Gay and Lesbian Youth*, pp. 1–42. New York: Harrington, 1989.

This is the introduction to the first general reader on the topic of gay and lesbian adolescence, with a number of selections that deal with aspects of family life and parent/child relations.

———. *Same Sex, Different Cultures.* New York: Westview, 1997.

This study is a short, cross-cultural study of the lives and issues confronting gay men and lesbians around the world, including aspects of culture, family, and community.

Herdt, G. and A. Boxer. *Children of Horizons: How Gay and Lesbian Youth Are Leading a New Way Out of the Closet.* Boston: Beacon, 1993.

The first comprehensive community and developmental study of the coming out process of adolescents in the United States. This study highlights aspects of change and resilience in the lives of individuals and families and is highly recommended for general readers and specialists.

Laird, Joan, and Robert-Jay Green, eds. *Lesbians and Gays in Couples and Families: A Handbook for Therapists.* San Francisco: Jossey-Bass, 1996.

Levine, Martin, Peter Nardi, and John Gagnon, eds. *In Changing Times.* Chicago: University of Chicago Press, 1996.

A comprehensive examination of the impact of the AIDS epidemic on the gay and lesbian community from some of the most significant observers and commentators of the past quarter century.

Marcus, Eric. *Is It a Choice? Answers to 300 of the Most Frequently Asked Questions About Gays and Lesbians.* San Francisco: HarperSanFrancisco, 1993.

Muller, Ann. *Parents Matter: Parents' Relationships with Lesbian Daughters and Gay Sons.* New York: Naiad, 1987.

The first detailed study of the stories and lives of parents of gays and lesbians as related by a mother of a gay son. The participants were largely derived from PFLAG. This is a compassionate and astute study with many good insights and is highly recommended.

Rafkin, Louise, ed. *Different Daughters: A Book by Mothers of Lesbians.* Pittsburgh: Cleis, 1996.

Ryan, Caitlin and Donna Futterman. *Lesbian and Gay Youth: Care and Counseling.* New York: Columbia University Press, 1997.

An award-winning comprehensive survey of the needs and resources for adolescent and young adult gays and lesbians and their families. The mental health discussions are particularly valuable for parents seeking answers to critical questions.

Notes

Introduction: When Your Child Says, "I Have Something to Tell You . . ."

1. Robb Forman Dew, *The Family Heart: A Memoir of When Our Son Came Out* (New York: Ballantine, 1994).
2. G. B. McDonald, "Exploring Sexual Identity: Gay People and Their Families," *Sex Education Coalition News*, no. 5, p. 1, quoted by Ritch C. Savin-Williams in "Coming Out to Parents and Self-Esteem Among Gay and Lesbian Youths," *Journal of Homosexuality* 18, nos. 1–2 (1989). A 1989 study demonstrated that gay males who see their parents' approval as important to their self-worth are more likely to have higher self-esteem if their homosexuality is accepted by their parents (Savin-Williams, "Coming Out to Parents," p. 30).
3. G. Herdt and A. M. Boxer, *Children of Horizons: How Gay and Lesbian Teens Are Leading a New Way Out of the Closet* (Boston: Beacon, 1993), p. 181.
4. Gary Ramafedi, James A. Farrow, and Robert W. Diesher, "Risk Factors for Attempted Suicide in Gay and Bisexual Youth," in *Psychological Perspectives on Lesbian and Gay Male Experiences*, eds. Linda D. Garnets and Douglas C. Kimmel (New York: Columbia University Press, 1993), p. 495.
5. Michelangelo Signorile, *Life Outside: The Signorile Report on Gay Men—Sex, Drugs, Muscles, and the Passages of Life* (New York: Harper Collins, 1997).

6. P. Gibson, *Gay Male and Lesbian Youth Suicide: Report of the Secretary's Task Force on Youth Suicide* (Washington D.C.: U.S. Government Printing Office, DHHS pub. no. ADM, 1989), 3:110–142.
7. National Conference of Catholic Bishops/United States Catholic Conference, Washington, D.C., February 16, 1998.

1. The Heterosexual Family Myth: How It Can Be Harmful

1. George Weinberg, *Society and the Healthy Homosexual* (New York: St. Martin's, 1972). See also Gilbert Herdt, "Introduction: Gay Youth, Emergent Identities, and Cultural Scenes at Home and Abroad," in *Homosexuality and Adolescence*, ed. G. Herdt (New York: Harrington, 1989), pp. 1–42.
2. Tirosch Adital Ben-Ari, "It's the Telling That Makes the Difference," in *Interpreting Experience: The Narrative Study of Lives*, eds. R. Josselson and Am Lielich (Thousand Oaks, Calif.: Sage, 1995), 3:153–172.
3. A. M. Boxer, J. A. Coo, and G. Herdt, "To Tell or Not to Tell: Patterns of Self-Disclosure to Mothers and Fathers Reported by Gay and Lesbian Youth," in *Parent-Child Relations Across the Lifespan*, ed. K. Pillemer and K. McCartney (New York: Oxford University Press, 1991), pp. 59–93. See also Caitlin Ryan and Donna Futterman, *Lesbian and Gay Youth: Care and Counseling* (New York: Columbia University Press, 1998); Anthony R. D'Augelli "Enhancing the Development of Lesbian, Gay, and Bisexual Youths," in *Preventing Heterosexism and Homophobia*, eds. E. D. Rothblum and L. A. Bond (Thousand Oaks, Calif.: Sage, 1995), pp. 124–150; Joyce Hunter and Robert Schaecher, "Gay and Lesbian Adolescents," in *Encyclopedia of Social Work*, 19th ed. (Washington, D.C.: NASW Press, 1994), pp. 1055–1063.
4. A. M. Boxer, B. Cohler, G. Herdt, and F. Irvin, "Gay and Lesbian Youth," in *Handbook of Clinical Research and Practice with Adolescents*, eds. P. H. Tolan and B. J. Cohler (New York: John Wiley, 1993), pp. 249–280. See also G. Herdt, "Developmental Continuity as a Dimension of Sexual Orientation Across Cultures," in *Homosexuality and Heterosexuality: The Kinsey Scale and Current Research*, eds. David McWhirter, J. Reinisch, and S. Sanders (New York: Oxford University Press, 1990), pp. 208–238; G. Herdt, " 'Coming Out' as a Rite of Passage: A Chicago Study," in *Gay Culture in America*, ed. G. Herdt (Boston: Beacon, 1992), pp. 29–67; G. Herdt and A. M. Boxer, "Epilogue: Growing Up Gay and Lesbian in the Time of AIDS," in G. Herdt and A. M. Boxer, *Children of Horizons* (Boston: Beacon, 1993).
5. Gilbert Herdt, *Same Sex, Different Cultures* (New York: Westview, 1997); John D'Emilio, *Sexual Politics, Sexual Communities: The Making of a Homosexual Minority in the United States, 1940–1970* (Chicago: University of Chicago Press, 1983).

2. What Affects a Family's Resilience?

1. Froma Walsh, *Strengthening Family Resilience* (New York and London: Guilford, 1998), p. 4.
2. Ibid., p. 6.
3. Gina O'Connell Higgins, *Resilient Adults: Overcoming a Cruel Past* (San Francisco: Jossey-Bass, 1994), p. 62.
4. Walsh, *Strengthening*, p. 133.
5. See, for example, Erik F. Strommen, "You're a What? Family Member Reactions to the Disclosure of Homosexuality," in *Psychological Perspectives of Lesbian and Gay Male Experiences*, eds. L. D. Garnetts and D. G. Kimmel (New York: Columbia University Press, 1993), esp. pp. 251–252.
6. Carol Gilligan, *In a Different Voice: Psychological Theory and Women's Development* (Cambridge: Harvard University Press, 1982); Nancy J. Chodorow, "Heterosexuality as a Compromise Formation: Reflections on the Psychoanalytic Theory of Sexual Development," *Psychoanalysis and Contemporary Thought* 15 (1992): 267–304.
7. Ellen Lewin, *Lesbian Mothers: Accounts of Gender in American Culture* (Ithaca, N.Y.: Cornell University Press, 1993); Charlotte J. Patterson, "Families of the Lesbian Baby Boom: Parents' Division of Labor and Children's Adjustment," *Developmental Psychology* 31 (1995): 115–123.
8. G. Herdt and A.M. Boxer, *Children of Horizons: How Gay and Lesbian Teens Are Leading a New Way Out of the Closet* (Boston: Beacon, 1993), p. 181.

3. When a Family Loses Its Way: Disintegration

1. G. Herdt and A. M. Boxer, *Children of Horizons: How Gay and Lesbian Teens Are Leading a New Way Out of the Closet* (Boston: Beacon, 1993), p. 228.
2. Kath Weston, *Families We Choose: Lesbians, Gays, Kinship* (New York: Columbia University Press, 1991). See also Joan Laird and R. Green, eds., *Lesbians and Gays in Couples and Families: A Handbook for Therapists* (San Francisco: Jossey-Bass, 1996).
3. As quoted in Caitlan Ryan and Donna Futterman, *Lesbian and Gay Youth: Care and Counseling* (New York: Columbia University Press, 1998), p. 64.
4. Ibid, p. 64.
5. Gilbert Herdt, *Gay and Lesbian Youth* (New York: Haworth, 1989). See also Boxer et al.
6. Martin S. Weinberg et al., *Dual Desires: Understanding Bisexuality* (New York: Oxford University Press, 1993).

4. Somewhere in the Middle: Ambivalence

1. Anne Muller, *Parents Matter: Parents' Relationships with Lesbian Daughters and Gay Sons* (New York: Naiad, 1987).
2. G. Herdt and A. M. Boxer, "Epilogue" to paperback edition of *Children of Horizons: How Gay and Lesbian Teens are Leading a New Way Out of the Closet* (Boston: Beacon, 1996); see also Martha McClintock and Gilbert Herdt, "Rethinking Puberty: The Development of Sexual Attraction," *Current Directions in Psychological Science* 5 (1996): 178–183, and Gilbert Herdt, *Same Sex, Different Cultures* (New York: Westview, 1997).
3. Richard Isay. *Becoming Gay: The Journey to Self-Acceptance* (New York: Pantheon, 1986).
4. Ellen Lewin, *Recognizing Ourselves: Ceremonies of Lesbian and Gay Commitment* (New York: Columbia University Press, 1998).

6. You Have Something to Hear: New Cultural Ideals

1. J. Boswell, *Christianity, Social Tolerance, and Homosexuality* (Chicago: University of Chicago Press, 1980); Frederick W. Bozett, "Gay and Lesbian Parents: Future Perspectives," in *Gay and Lesbian Parents*, ed. F. W. Bozett (New York: Praeger, 1987), pp. 231–237; J. D'Emilio and E. B. Freedman, *Intimate Matters: A History of Sexuality in America* (New York: Harper and Row, 1988); John Gagnon and W. Simon, *Sexual Conduct* (Chicago: Aldine, 1973); David Greenberg, *The Construction of Homosexuality* (Chicago: University of Chicago Press, 1988); Gilbert Herdt, ed., *Gay Culture in America* (Boston: Beacon, 1992); J. Weeks, *Sexuality and Its Discontents* (London: Routledge and Kegan Paul, 1985).
2. Paul Robinson, *The Modernization of Sex: Havelock Ellis, Alfred Kinsey, William Masters, and Virginia Johnson* (Ithaca, N.Y.: Cornell University Press, 1976).
3. I. Beiber et al., *Homosexuality: A Psychoanalytic Study* (New York: Basic Books, 1962). For the most recent detailed analyses, see Robert P. Cabaj and Terry S. Stein, eds., *Textbook of Homosexuality and Mental Health* (Washington, D.C.: American Psychiatric Association Press, 1996).
4. Gilbert Herdt, *The Sambia: Ritual and Gender in New Guinea* (New York: Holt, Reinhart and Winston, 1987). See also Gilbert Herdt, *Same Sex, Different Cultures* (New York: Westview, 1997).
5. Clelland S. Ford and Frank A. Beach, *Patterns of Sexual Behavior* (New York: Harper and Row, 1951).
6. Evelyn Hooker, "The Adjustment of the Male Overt Homosexual," *Journal of Projective Techniques* 21 (1957): 18–31.

7. Gilbert Herdt and Andrew M. Boxer, "Introduction: Culture, History, and Life Course of Gay Men," in *Gay Culture in America*, ed. G. Herdt (Boston: Beacon, 1992), pp. 1–28.

8. See Cabaj and Stein, eds., *Textbook of Homosexuality*.

9. Timothy Murphy, "Redirecting Sexual Orientations: Techniques and Justifications" *Journal of Sex Research* 29 (1992): 501–523.

Index

Judith Roof, *Come As You Are: Sexuality and Narrative*

Terry Castle, *Noel Coward and Radclyffe Hall: Kindred Spirits*

Kath Weston, *Render Me, Gender Me: Lesbians Talk Sex, Class, Color, Nation, Studmuffins . . .*

Ruth Vanita, *Sappho and the Virgin Mary: Same-Sex Love and the English Literary Imagination*

renée c. hoogland, *Lesbian Configurations*

Beverly Burch, *Other Women: Lesbian Experience and Psychoanalytic Theory of Women*

Jane McIntosh Snyder, *Lesbian Desire in the Lyrics of Sappho*

Rebecca Alpert, *Like Bread on the Seder Plate: Jewish Lesbians and the Transformation of Tradition*

Emma Donoghue, editor, *Poems Between Women: Four Centuries of Love, Romantic Friendship, and Desire*

James T. Sears and Walter L. Williams, editors, *Overcoming Heterosexism and Homophobia: Strategies That Work*

Patricia Juliana Smith, *Lesbian Panic: Homoeroticism in Modern British Women's Fiction*

Dwayne C. Turner, *Risky Sex: Gay Men and HIV Prevention*

Timothy F. Murphy, *Gay Science: The Ethics of Sexual Orientation Research*

Cameron McFarlane, *The Sodomite in Fiction and Satire, 1660–1750*

Lynda Hart, *Between the Body and the Flesh: Performing Sadomasochism*

Byrne R. S. Fone, editor, *The Columbia Anthology of Gay Literature: Readings from Western Antiquity to the Present Day*

Ellen Lewin, *Recognizing Ourselves: Ceremonies of Lesbian and Gay Commitment*

Ruthann Robson, *Sappho Goes to Law School: Fragments in Lesbian Legal Theory*

Jacquelyn Zita, *Body Talk: Philosophical Reflections on Sex and Gender*

Evelyn Blackwood and Saskia Wieringa, *Female Desires: Same-Sex Relations and Transgender Practices Across Cultures*

Marilee Lindemann, *Willa Cather: Queering America*

George E. Haggerty, *Men in Love: Masculinity and Sexuality in the Eighteenth Century*

Andrew Elfenbein, *Romantic Genius: The Prehistory of a Homosexual Role*

Gilbert Herdt and Bruce Koff, *Something to Tell You: The Road Families Travel When a Child Is Gay*

Richard Canning, *Gay Fiction Speaks: Conversations with Gay Novelists*

Laura Doan, *Fashioning Sapphism: The Origins of a Modern English Lesbian Culture*